Contemporary Male Spirituality

A MAN AND HIS GOD

Martin W. Pable, OFM Cap.

AVE MARIA PRESS Notre Dame, IN 46556

Acknowledgments

Scripture texts used in this work are taken from The New American Bible
with Revised New Testament, copyright © 1986 by the Confraternity of
Christian Doctrine, Washington, D.C. and are used with permission. All
rights reserved.

Source for the quotes from the documents of the Second Vatican Council is
Vatican Council II, Austin Flannery, O.P. General Editor (Collegeville,
MN: The Liturgical Press, 1975).

Material used with permission from *The Ministry of the Celebrating Community* by Rev. Eugene Walsh. (The booklet may be obtained from Pastoral
Arts Associates, 642 N. Grandview, Daytona Beach, FL 32018.)

International Standard Book Number: 0-87793-380-4

Library of Congress Catalog Card Number: 88-71083

Printed and bound in the United States of America.

To all the men who have shared the joys and struggles, the hopes and anxieties of their life-journey with me; and in a special way to Dick and Margie Schwebel, who inspired and encouraged me to write this book.

Contents

Preface 7

Chapter 1 What Is Spirituality? 11

Chapter 2 Getting the Vision 27

Chapter 3 Who Am I? 43

Chapter 4 The World of Work and Leisure 59

Chapter 5 The Quest for Love 73

Chapter 6 A Man and His Responsibilities 95

Chapter 7 Continuing Spiritual Growth 121

Suggested Resources 143

Preface

It was a wintry Saturday afternoon in Racine, Wisconsin. One of the parishes had asked me to conduct a day of recollection on social justice. I suppose there were 30 to 40 people there. What I remember most vividly about the day was the coffee break. During my presentation I had talked a bit about how I saw justice issues emerging in my pastoral counseling ministry. I had seen the negative impact of oppression and discrimination against women, I said. But, I added, I have also seen what damage cultural pressures in our society can do to men. Many men are faced with a double set of expectations. At work they are expected to be aggressive, competitive and unfeeling; when they come home, they are expected to be affectionate, tuned in to their emotional side and sensitive to the feelings of spouse and children.

During the break a couple of men came up to me and said, "You really hit on something there. You know, our wives go on a retreat every year and they're always telling us how much it does for them. Do you suppose you could do a retreat for a bunch of us guys?" By this time some wives had joined our group and were nodding vigorously. "O.K.," I said. "If you can get the men, I'll provide the time and place."

It took about six months, but we stuck with it. In the fall we gathered, ten laymen and myself, in a house facing Lake Michigan. We began by watching a video on midlife transitions, then started to share our own journeys. By Saturday night we were sitting around the fireplace and talking about sex. Then, as if it were a perfectly natural transition, one of the men said, "Marty, tell us about how you pray." We continued long into the night, sharing our struggles with prayer, with faith and with doubt. We had bonded at the level

of spirit. The next morning, during Sunday liturgy, we discussed together how we could continue to support one another in our spiritual
life after we left the retreat.

Because we were all busy men, we were not too successful in our
resolve. However, we did organize another retreat for the following
fall. This time we had 15 men, so we decided to go to a diocesan retreat center which had more room and regular food service. I remember being deeply touched by the sharing that took place that
weekend. One man was trying to keep his marriage from breaking
up; another one's wife was battling with a terminal illness; many of
them were dealing with problems in their jobs or in the lives of their
children. As we prayed together, I don't think I have ever experienced such heart-felt prayer rising out of the lives of flesh-and-blood
men, some of whom were not practicing Catholics in the orthodox
sense. This time the bonding was so strong that we committed ourselves to meet once a month, at 8 a.m. on Saturday morning (these
guys were motivated!), to pray together and fill each other in on how
we were doing. The wives began calling us "Marty's Men." We stuck
to our covenant for a whole year. And even after I was transferred
out of state, the men continued their monthly get-togethers. We have
had two more retreats since then, each attended by a larger group.
These groups are continuing to meet on a regular basis.

It is out of these experiences that this book was born. It has been
nurtured further by my experience of listening to the many men who
came for retreats at Queen of Angels Retreat in Saginaw, Michigan.
Recently I saw an article entitled "Real Men Do Have a Spirituality."
That, indeed, is what I have learned. It is still a cultural bias that
things like prayer, religion and spirituality are for women only. I am
willing to admit that there may be something in the feminine psyche
that readily disposes women toward things of the spirit. But my experience tells me that there is an increasing number of men who are drawn
toward a deeper spiritual life, indeed do have a spirituality. But they
do not always recognize it for what it is. Some are embarrassed by the
attraction, some repress it, some pursue it by way of fundamentalism.
And some are fortunate enough to find nourishment for it in the scriptures and in the rich spiritual tradition of the church.

It is for these men (as well as the women in their lives) that these
pages are written. If they prove to be a guide for anyone's spiritual
journey, I shall feel richly rewarded.

I want to express my heartfelt gratitude to the men and women who have shared their lives and their struggles with me and have encouraged me to write this book. In a special way I wish to thank my typists, Betty Southgate and Ann Laundra, for their patience and dedication in preparing the manuscript for publication.

Martin W. Pable, OFM Cap.

1

What Is Spirituality?

The word "spirituality" can be a turnoff for some men today. To them it sounds like woman-talk. To others it resurrects memories of boring catechism classes and church services. To others it just isn't relevant to the real world of computers, marketing research and growth curves.

So let's leave behind the churchy language and images for awhile. Instead of asking "What is spirituality?" let's ask a different question: "What is a human being?" The obvious answer is that a human being is a two-legged animal who eats, sleeps, mates, builds, destroys and eventually dies. But we all recognize that there are some things about humans that are different from the other animals. Humans laugh and cry. They feel (at least at times) a sense of responsibility for their choices. They can feel guilt about the past and anxiety about the future. They are capable of making commitments and standing by them even at great cost to themselves. And they are capable of cruelty, violence and torture far surpassing even the most savage beasts of the animal kingdom.

There is something else that is curiously different about human beings. They ask questions. Not just factual questions like, "What time is it?" but questions about the very nature of reality. Every man who is a father will recognize the following dialogue:

Child: "Daddy, why does it get dark at night?"
Dad: "Because the sun goes down."
Child: "Where does it go?"
Dad: "It moves to the other side of the earth."
Child: "Why, Dad?"

As the child grows up, the questions become more complex:

• Where do babies come from?

- Why are some people good and others bad?
- Why do people make war?
- What happens to us after death?
- Why are we in this world in the first place?

To be human, then, is to ask questions about the most profound issues: the origin of the universe, the nature of truth and love, the meaning and purpose of life. Another distinctly human trait is the capacity for wonder. We have all seen the wide-eyed, open-mouthed look of the child when he or she spots the shiny new bike under the Christmas tree. The look is usually followed by an exclamation: "Wow!" We all know what it means. We had the same experience when we saw our first space rocket blast-off on television. It's wonder.

Let me share with you a few of my own experiences of wonder. A couple of years ago I was watching one of the Nova programs on television. This one happened to be about sperm swimming around and finally uniting with a female egg. There were actual photographs of the embryo developing within the womb. We were able to see not only the tiny limbs but even some of the internal organs of a developing human being. There were a good number of us watching that program together, but I can still remember the hushed silence in the room when it was over. A feeling of wonder and mystery had come over all of us.

I remember the time I was writing Christmas cards and I happened to be listening to Beethoven's Seventh Symphony at the same time. All of a sudden I got totally absorbed in the music. I was awestruck as I wondered how such incredibly beautiful music could come from a man whose personal life was so lonely and scarred by physical and mental suffering.

Another time I was driving along the freeway at night. It had been a long day and I was getting drowsy. Suddenly I heard an awful noise. It was my car going off onto the gravel shoulder of the road. I barely managed to turn the wheel to keep from going into the ditch. After I had calmed down I again felt that deep sense of wonder. What if the car had drifted into the left lane? I would have been hit from behind. What if I had slammed into a bridge or an abutment? Why was my life spared? The illusion of having all control over my life was dispelled in that instant. I was brought into vivid contact with the utter frailty of human life.

Sense of Mystery

Contemporary theologians like Karl Rahner and John Shea call these experiences "encounters with Mystery." We intuitively sense that there is something beyond the boundaries of our own ego, even beyond the collective egos of the rest of humankind. There is a presence and a power in the universe that is somehow addressing us. On our side, the fact that we keep wondering and asking questions about meaning, purpose and the ultimate reveals our capacity for reaching beyond ourselves. Theologians call this "self-transcendence."

Now, a crucial question: Is this wondering and questioning of ours finally in vain? Is "the encounter with Mystery" nothing but a projection of our own wishes for a parent-figure or some other form of security? "Yes," would be the answer of Freud and other skeptics and agnostics. "There really is nothing 'out there.' This is the only world there is, the only life there is, and the only noble thing to do is to accept it and make the best of it."

On the other hand, religious people refuse to believe that their experience of transcendence is only a projection of their mind or a consequence of eating last night's garlic and onions. They accept the existence of the mystery, and they even give it a name: God. Moreover, they believe that this God is not indifferent to them. Rather, God is calling them into personal relationship with himself. But now we are getting ahead of our story.

First, I invite you to reflect on your own experiences of wonder, mystery and transcendence. Where have you sensed the holy, the presence of God in human life?

- Was it when you knelt at Benediction as a boy and smelled the incense and watched the candles and somehow knew you were in the holy presence of God?

- Was it that day you played the perfect game, didn't make any mistakes and felt convinced you were being helped by a power beyond yourself?

- Was it the first time you heard the heart-beat of your first baby in your wife's body?

- Was it after that stormy period in your life when you and she looked back and said, "We could never have made it without God!"

- Was it the day your teenage daughter, who hadn't done a lick of work around the house in light years, suddenly said, "Looks like you and Mom need a break; I'll clean the house this weekend!"

Karl Rahner would claim that religious experiences can occur even if "God" is not explicitly recognized in them. The essence of religious experience is that it nudges us to wonder and to ask the deeper questions. It happens, for example, whenever we find someone hanging on to hope even when most others have given up; whenever a person keeps loving even though their love is not returned; whenever someone forgives a terrible injury committed against him or her; whenever one continues to stand up for the truth, even at the risk of great personal loss. All these situations confront the human observer with the inexorable questions: Why? What motivates them? What is the secret of their endurance, their commitment, their serenity in the face of personal suffering?

Note, however, that none of these experiences, or all of them together, can absolutely prove the existence of God. I am reminded of the great story told by the Jewish theologian Martin Buber. A scientist-agnostic went to visit the Rabbi Levi Jizchak in order to argue with him and try to shatter his old-fashioned beliefs. He found the rabbi pacing up and down in his room with a book in his hand. At first the rabbi paid no attention to his visitor. But suddenly he stopped, looked at the scholar and said, "But perhaps it is true after all!" The scholar didn't know what to say. The rabbi continued, "My son, the great scholars of the Bible with whom you have argued have wasted their words on you; you laughed at them when you left. They were unable to lay God and his kingdom on the table before you; and neither can I. But think, my son, perhaps it is true after all!" As the story goes, this great "perhaps" stuck in the scientist's mind until he too became a believer.

The point I wish to make, though, is that no one "can lay God and his kingdom on the table" before us like irrefutable truth in a court trial. The fact is, both belief and unbelief are *choices*. Both are "a leap in the dark." Both are made with doubt and hesitation. The atheist cannot prove that our faith is groundless, but neither can we prove the absolute validity of our faith.

From now on, I am going to assume that you, my readers, are people of faith. Or at least that you are struggling with questions of belief. It is good to recall that faith can indeed coexist with doubt and with questioning. As John Powell has said, God allows us to struggle with our questions so that we can live into the answers. In my years of counseling and spiritual direction, I have heard believers question just about every one of the teachings of the Bible and of the Catholic faith. In practically every instance, as I walked through this difficult time with them, they either came to a more mature understanding of their beliefs or learned to live peacefully with mysteries that no human mind can fully comprehend.

It might seem as though we have strayed far from our opening question: What is spirituality? But in reality we have not. We have been trying to lay a foundation for a spirituality based on our own human experience. Otherwise, our spirituality will be split off from the rest of life, and that is a mistake that Christians have made all too often. Spirituality, I think, is a powerful source of energy. But if it is going to give us direction and motivation, it has to touch us in our everyday lives.

I would say, then, that *spirituality is first of all a quest*. If it is true that we human beings are questioners, this also implies that we are seekers. What are we seeking? The ancient Christian philosophers used to answer: Our mind seeks the truth and our heart seeks the good. Something tells us, though, that we will never be satisfied with partial truth or partial goodness. We always want to know more, and we always want to possess more of what seems good. We discover within ourselves a capacity for the infinite.

One of the stunning beliefs of the Christian faith is that the infinite God is also in search of us. We have absolutely no idea why. If the word "God" means anything at all, it implies that he possesses all perfection. He clearly does not need human creatures for his own completeness. But the relentless testimony of the Bible is that God has a foolishly uncontrollable desire to share his life and being with us. Theologians call this "God's self-communication to us." Another word for it is "grace." And it is this relationship with God that is the foundation of spirituality. In fact, a simple but good definition of spirituality would be: the ongoing endeavor to grow in our relationship with God.

Divine Initiative

But before we develop this notion any further, we need to be very clear about something: Left to ourselves, we would probably never develop a relationship with God. While it is true that all of us

have the capacity for the infinite, we all too easily try to satisfy ourselves with the finite. The world of the immediate, the tangible, the
pleasurable is much more enticing than the invisible world of the
spiritual. Moreover, the signals we receive from our spiritual nature
are weak in comparison. We do indeed have our moments of wonder
and of questioning, but it is relatively easy to ignore them. We have
an uncanny ability to suppress those signals from our spiritual self
and to get on with the business of making a living and having a little
fun. I recall a British movie of the '60s called *Bedazzled*. It was about
an ordinary fellow working in a hamburger joint and living a humdrum existence. One day the devil appears and says he will grant him
any three wishes provided he gives the devil control of his life. Each
time the hero makes his wish the devil grants it, but in exaggerated
form. And each time the hero begs him to take back the wish. In the
end, he returns to his humdrum hamburger joint. At one level, the
movie is a delightfully funny comedy. But at a deeper level, it's a profound parable about our own human condition. We indeed long for
something beyond ordinariness, but we keep getting "bedazzled" by
whatever society happens to define as the good life. So we miss the
transcendent mystery, the God who alone can fill the empty spot in
our soul. We will be talking more about this in Chapter 2.

My point right now is this: It is God who bridges the gap. It is
God who takes the initiative in the divine-human encounter. Christians have always believed that we are incapable of saving ourselves,
however we define "salvation." But the deeper truth is: We could not
even take the first step toward God if he in his goodness did not first
stretch out his hand to us. It is "not that we have loved God," St. John
says, "but that he has loved us" (1 Jn 4:10).

This truth appears on practically every page of the Bible. The
first pages of Genesis reveal the original familiarity of Adam and Eve
with God. But then, after the Fall, the couple goes into hiding. At
this point we need to imagine a profound, almost terrifying silence in
paradise. Nobody is talking. God is taking his usual walk in the garden in the cool "breezy time of the day" (Gn 3:8), but he is alone.
Adam and Eve are also alone, hiding among the trees. They are not
talking either, because they are guilty and afraid. Think of it—that
awful silence could have continued right down to the present. The
only one who could have broken through the silence was God. That's
why I've always thought that Genesis 3:9 is the original "good news"

of the scriptures: "The LORD God then called to the man and asked him, 'Where are you?'" The question unmasks the deceit of the sinful pair, but at the same time it offers hope. God has not given up on his human creatures. He is willing to begin a new dialogue. This scene is the prototype for all God's initiatives in scripture:

"Abraham, Abraham!" (Gn 22:1).

"Moses! Moses!" (Ex 3:4).

"The word of the LORD came to me [Jeremiah] thus: . . ." (Jer 1:4).

"In times past, God spoke in fragmentary and varied ways to our fathers through the prophets; in this, the final age, he has spoken to us through his Son" (Heb 1:1).

Indeed, we Christians believe that Jesus Christ is God's ultimate self-communication. The mystery of the incarnation, as the church calls it, is God's most intimate breakthrough into human history, his most loving initiative. "Yes, God so loved the world that he gave his only Son" (Jn 3:16). The gospel pages are filled with instances of Jesus continuing the pattern of divine initiative. In the very beginning of Jesus' public life, John the Baptist points him out to two of his disciples. The two begin to follow Jesus, who suddenly turns around and asks them, "What are you looking for?" (Jn 1:38).

It would be good for us to pause and reflect on these and similar questions that God addresses to us in the scriptures. They are the questions that other people never or seldom put to us, and that we ourselves would just as soon avoid. Yet we hear them in the depths of our spirit, and they cannot be ignored once they are heard.

—"Where are you?" (Gn 3:9). This is not a question of geography but of selfhood. Where do I stand? What am I grounded in? What are my deepest commitments? Where is my life leading?

—"What are you looking for?" (Jn 1:38) Not a shopping question but a goal question. What is missing in my life? What is it that I really want? What am I trying to achieve by all my flurry of activities?

—"Do you want to be healed?" Jesus asks the crippled man (Jn 5:6). To me the question might be: What do I need to be healed of? What is my sickness? What is paralyzing me, blocking me from my goals?

—"What do you want me to do for you?" Jesus asks the blind man (Mk 10:51). A very good question for me. Am I trying to be Mr.

Independent, trying to do it all by myself? Do I really believe that Christ has the power and the will to do something for me? What is it that I truly need?

This, then, is the first movement of spirituality: God inviting us into friendship with himself. I have long ago given up trying to figure out why God would do such an outlandish thing. I've decided that that question is irrelevant. The only relevant question is: *What kind of response am I going to make?* That is the second movement of spirituality. I fear, though, that too often we have put too much emphasis on this second movement. We have stressed the "you gotta" approach: Spirituality means "you gotta" pray more, go to church more, give more of your money and time to God, and quit all your crummy habits. That's enough to discourage anyone. Spirituality ought to be a positive, life-giving endeavor. The only way it can be is to give priority to the activity of God. Once we begin to experience the power of God, the guidance of God, the healing of God, the love of God breaking into our lives, we will want to respond. At some point we will surrender our life to him. In other words, we will make a commitment. From our side, that is the beginning of a spiritual life.

Types of Christians

How does that happen to people? Let me share with you a few typical patterns that I have observed in my own experience. In the first place, I have met a good number of what I call "cradle-to-adult" Christians. That is, people who were baptized and brought up in a healthy Christian environment. For as long as they can remember, they felt God close to them. They eagerly accepted Jesus Christ as their Lord and tried to put his teachings into practice. Often they were not very vocal about their faith, but it was evident in the way they lived. They may never have made a deliberate, conscious act of commitment to Christ, but it was implicit in their whole lifestyle.

I remember a man in his late 30s who was telling me about the involvements he and his wife have in their parish. Among other things, they have been taking in Asiatic refugee children in addition to their own three. The other day, he said, one of the refugee boys asked them why they were doing so much for children who weren't even theirs. Mike told me very simply, "We explained that we felt this was the best way we can live out the teachings of Jesus. He taught us to love everyone, especially children." Mike has had no dramatic conversion experience. He was not "born again." He has been a practicing Catholic all his life. The grace of his baptism, nourished by prayer, the Eucharist and the church's liturgical life, has brought him to a mature, adult level of Christian spirituality.

Another form of spiritual awakening is what I call the "lost-and-found" Christian. People in this category typically have experienced a Christian upbringing, often including parochial school and regular participation in the sacraments. But at some point, during high school or soon after, they went through a period of drifting away or even rebellion. They quit praying and going to church. They may even have ridiculed their former beliefs and practices. They never formally renounced their Catholicism, but neither did they practice it.

Then, something happens to jar them. As one man told me, he met a Catholic girl who turned down his sexual advances and told him he needed to go to confession. Enough to jar anybody! He said he wasn't ready for that step yet, but he began to see that his life had become quite shallow. "I still remembered my Catholic upbringing," he said, "and I knew I had something to go back to." Before long he came back to the sacraments and got married in the church.

For a lot of other men, their spiritual indifference lasts a longer time. They may agree to a church wedding to pacify their bride and their parents, but there is no real commitment of faith. Some years later, half sensing a spiritual void, they let themselves be talked into attending a retreat, a Marriage Encounter, or a Bible Study group. The experience does not simply reawaken repressed childhood religion; rather, a whole new vision opens out. "I never realized what my faith was all about," the man will say. Or, "This is the first time I've ever met real Christians." Which is not exactly true, of course, but it is the first time he has paused long enough to look and listen. One man told me it was the witness of a deeply Christian businessman that brought him back to his own Christian roots. Whatever the process that led up to it, these men experience a certain feeling of "coming home." And they begin to develop a genuine spirituality.

A third group who have opened up to spirituality are what I call the "up-from-crisis" Christians. These are men who have bottomed out, have run out of answers, have teetered on the brink of despair. Some are recovering alcoholics or drug abusers. Some, like Ken, are overachievers who have spent all their lives running in the fast track.

Eventually Ken burned out and ended up in the psychiatric hospital. In the course of treatment he got in touch with his own spiritual emptiness and decided to "quit trying to play God." Sharing scripture with a small group of Christians and regaining his lost faith were crucial factors in his recovery.

Sometimes the crisis takes a long time to work through. Here is part of a letter I received from one man at the end of a retreat: "Two years ago at my first retreat here I was on an emotional rock bottom. It was hard to follow the minimum rules . . . and I had trouble sleeping. I asked for healing and for the strength to continue on my job. A year later (when I came on retreat) those prayers had been answered. I slept better but still craved excitement, thinking it had something to do with the Spirit. I prayed for the grace to be a better husband and father, and to forgive my wife for a situation that had arisen. Those prayers too have been answered. . . . This year I slept very well, and I'm praying for the ability to express love visibly, outside of being provider and live-in companion. I'll let you know next year how that has been fulfilled." Here one gets a glimpse of how "up-from-crisis" people often have to struggle toward the goal of spiritual growth.

There are all sorts of variations on these patterns, of course. The point is, all spirituality begins as a response to the experience of God inviting us into relationship. For some the invitation is a gentle nudge; for others it is a persistent tapping in the depths of the soul; for still others, it is a shaking of their very foundations. Our response takes the form of some kind of commitment, some act of surrender of our entire being. There are examples of this all through the scriptures. When Jesus and the apostles were discussing what people were saying about him, he suddenly threw the question straight at them: "And you—who do you say that I am?" There was an awkward moment of silence; then Simon Peter made his daring profession of faith: "You are the Messiah, the Son of the living God!" (Mt 16:16). When Thomas, skeptical about the resurrection stories, saw the risen Christ with the nail wounds in his body, he fell to his knees and said, "My Lord and my God!" (Jn 20:28). On the road to Damascus, Saul the persecutor recognized the glorified Christ in the blinding light and cried out, "What is it I must do?" (Acts 22:10).

As sudden and dramatic as these acts of commitment might seem, it is more likely that they were the outcome of a much longer process that psychologist William James called "subconscious incubation." That is, the human mind often silently "scans" the data long before making a judgment about it, and the will wavers back and forth before coming to decision. We can easily imagine, for example, that Paul was deeply impressed by the fearless speech of the martyr Stephen before the Jewish Sanhedrin, as well as by his courageous acceptance of death for the sake of Christ (Acts 7:54-60). No doubt he had been pondering all this long before the flash of light. Malcolm X, the black activist, said that while he was in prison he read the entire Bible and was convinced of the truth of its message. But it took him a whole week of interior struggle before he was able to kneel down and surrender his life to Jesus Christ. So, too, our own commitment is generally, I believe, the outcome of a longer process of which we are not fully aware and in which God himself is the principal agent.

Personal Commitment

We have been saying that the first movement of spirituality is that gracious invitation of God appealing to something deep within ourselves, and that the second movement is our response. We have seen that the response begins when we start to pay attention to our own feeling of dissatisfaction, restlessness, or whatever it is that tells us there is something missing in our lives. The response deepens when we come to the realization that we need God, that we cannot possibly be happy or fulfilled without him. We may have believed that as an abstract truth somewhere in our head, but now the conviction moves to the center of our being. We still are not sure what it all involves, but we find ourselves wanting to make some kind of commitment or surrender to God. Let's look more closely now at this "commitment" business.

Perhaps you have seen the famous painting of Christ carrying a lantern in one hand and knocking on a door with the other. The painting is based on a line in Revelation, the last book of the Bible: "Behold, I stand at the door and knock. If anyone hears my voice and opens the door [then] I will enter his house and dine with him, and he with me" (Rv 3:20). The door is a symbol of the human heart. Notice again who takes the initiative. It is Jesus who comes knocking and calling to us. In the painting, everyone notices that the door has no knob or latch on the outside. The artist is trying to express an important truth: Christ will never force his way into our lives. It is we who must open the door of our heart to him, which can only be done from the inside—that is, from our own free will. But if we make that choice, Jesus says, he will come in and share a meal with us. To share a meal in the Middle East is always a sign of special friendship. Once again we are back to the very essence of spirituality: a personal relationship with Jesus Christ.

Commitment then is that act of opening the door of our heart to Christ and receiving the gift of friendship that he offers us. If we were baptized as infants, we believe that the relationship with him began then. That beautiful sacrament took us right into the heart of God. We became sons of the Father, brothers of Jesus Christ, and living temples of the Holy Spirit. And that all happened, not because we had done anything to deserve it (we were barely conscious!) but simply because " . . . God chose us in Christ, before the foundation of the world," as St. Paul says (Eph 1:4). However, at some point each of us needs to make a conscious decision to receive God's gift as an adult. Some of us do that at our confirmation. Others are moved to it at the time of a retreat, or when we're reading the Bible, or at some unpredictable moment of our lives. We find ourselves saying something like, "Lord Jesus, whatever it means, I want to surrender myself to you. I don't want to live just for myself. I want you to be at the center of my life. I accept your gift of friendship, and I ask you to help me to live as you want me to."

Some people call this being "born again," but I don't particularly like that expression. Catholic Christians believe they are reborn in baptism. But if being born again means making an adult commitment to Jesus Christ, then it has meaning for me. I have great respect for Christians who say they are born again; but I resent it when they tell me I can't be saved unless I have the same experience they did. There are many different ways of coming to form a personal relationship with Christ. In fact, I think most of us have to renew our commitment to him more than once in our lifetime.

Many of us have heard the TV evangelists call for commitment. "Bow your heads now in prayer," they say, "and invite the Lord Jesus into your heart. And if you feel his Spirit moving you to make your commitment, come on down here and stand before the altar. Let everyone see that you accept Jesus Christ as your Lord and Savior." It can be a powerful moment, even on television. I have no doubt that the people who come forward are sincere in their conviction. For some it may represent a deep personal conversion that is lasting. For many, however, I don't believe it is lasting, for the simple reason that an experience like that needs to be nourished and reinforced in an ongoing way. There is just too much else competing for that person's time, energy and loyalty. Without ongoing support and nourishment, a few days or weeks in our supercharged world are enough to push Jesus Christ back to the periphery of consciousness.

By the same token, I have found too many "cradle Catholics" who never made a personal commitment to Christ. They were taught that their spiritual life can be nourished by reciting memorized prayers, receiving the sacraments and doing a few good works. These are not bad men, mind you. They are often hard-working, responsible, basically good family men. They attend Sunday Mass regularly and may even go to confession once or twice a year. But there is no heart, no enthusiasm in their religion. It is like a separate compartment that never influences the other compartments of their lives. They are not involved in their parish, apart from helping to set up booths at the annual fall festival. Knowledge of their religion remains at the elementary or high school level. They are forever attending courses and workshops to improve themselves on their jobs, but they never think of doing something similar in regard to their Christianity. These men belong to the vast army of Sunday Catholics, dutifully plodding along on the road to salvation.

What happens, then, when a man commits himself to Jesus Christ, when he asks Christ to come into his life as his Lord and Savior? In the first place, provided his request is sincere, Christ will always grant it. Remember what we said before: Our God is even more eager to share his life with us than we are to receive it. When we respond to his initiative, he comes to us with the fullness of his gifts.

According to the Bible, the greatest gift that Christ wants to give us is the Holy Spirit. He promised the Spirit to the disciples at the Last Supper, and he fulfilled the promise at Pentecost. Most of us are aware of the remarkable changes that took place in the apostles after Pentecost. Men who were full of doubts and fears became incredibly bold in speaking of their convictions. Men who shrank from any conflict or opposition were willing to risk ridicule, hostility and even imprisonment for what they believed. Men who got hung up with petty quarrels among themselves formed communities of believers who took care of one another. The Acts of the Apostles is the story of what happens when people are touched by the power of the Holy Spirit.

What we don't seem to believe deeply enough is that this life-transforming power is available to modern-day Christians. People have confided in me some of the wonderful things that began to happen to them when they opened themselves to Christ and his gift of the Holy Spirit. They come to know God's presence and love in a new way, a personal way: "I guess I knew a lot *about* God," they say, "but now I know *him*." They experience Jesus Christ as their friend, walking with them, guiding them in their decisions, strengthening them in their times of stress. They find it easy to talk to him in prayer. The words of the scriptures take on new meaning. Instead of worrying about their problems, they sense a deep peace and confidence in the Lord's power to help them. Even their limitations and mistakes don't seem so horrendous any more, because they feel loved and accepted in a radical way.

Empowered by the presence of Christ and the gifts of the Holy Spirit, a man is now ready for the third movement of spirituality: He begins to form a vision and a lifestyle in line with his commitment. That is, instead of keeping separate compartments, he begins to make connections—first in his mind, then in his choices. He begins to ask new questions such as: How does God view this issue? What is his plan for marriage and family life? How does my job fit into his larger purposes for me and for the world? How does he see my children and my present style of parenting? What does Christ teach about human relations and dealing with difficult people? And instead of relying on his own insights and judgments, the man seeks guidance through prayer, reading the Bible and other spiritual sources, and the reflections of other faith-filled people. As he grows in vision, he also comes to see that his actions and choices need to be brought into line; otherwise, spirituality is little more than another head-trip. Here is where the going can get tough, because he may reach the conclusion that he has to make some changes in his lifestyle if he is going to be faithful to the new-found vision. As one fellow told me, "Spirituality was fun until I realized it meant giving God the right to ask some things of me!"

Let's be very clear about this. Spirituality is not meant to be fun-and-games. It's discipline, and it's tough. We Americans have an almost infinite capacity to trivialize everything, or at least to make it fit into our comfort zone. I recall walking into a bookstore in California (where else?) and heading for the Religion section. The first book that caught my eye had a title which spoke volumes about our national mind-set: *The Lazy Man's Guide to Spiritual Enlightenment.* That says it all. Even the spiritual life can be adapted to a flabby population!

I found it interesting that in November of 1985, George Gallup, Jr. celebrated the 50th anniversary of the famous Gallup Poll (begun by his father) by speaking to church leaders in Omaha on how to deepen America's spiritual commitment. Gallup was obviously concerned about this. He told the leaders that his latest report, "Religion in America," led him to the conclusion that "Americans have not turned to Jesus Christ in any widespread or profound way." While a huge majority—81 percent—consider themselves Christians, there is little evidence that their belief in Christ makes any significant impact on the way they live. As Gallup put it, Americans are "long on religion but short on morality." "We dutifully attend church," he said, "but are no less likely than our unchurched brethren to engage in unethical behavior. We say we rejoice in the 'good news' that Jesus brought, but are strangely reluctant to share the Gospel with others." Still, Gallup found some reason for hope in his finding that at least half of Americans wish their religious faith were stronger. If that wish could be nurtured and transformed into genuine commitment, America might experience a real spiritual awakening. It sounded a lot like what Jesus said in his conclusion to the Sermon on the Mount: "None of those who cry out 'Lord, Lord,' will enter the kingdom of God, but only the one who does the will of my Father in heaven" (Mt 7:21). Religion cannot remain a matter of ideas and words; it has to spill over into actions and choices.

But if spirituality is not for the flabby, neither is it meant to be a drag. Spirituality is basically, as we have seen, a relationship; and relationships are anything but dull—especially when one of the partners is the mysterious God. As C.S. Lewis once said, "You can't tame God. He's wild, you know." Not in the sense of being fierce or hostile, but in that he is full of surprises. He will not allow us to domesticate him or pull him into our complacent routines. At the same time, he is a God who understands our weaknesses and will not push us beyond our capacity.

What I am saying is that spirituality is anything but pious and sappy. It has the potential to energize us, to draw power out of us, to bring substance and direction into our lives. The rest of this book will focus on those two notions of vision and lifestyle. The underlying question will always be: If I commit myself to God and allow him to be the center of my life, what difference will it make? How will spirituality affect the way I feel about myself? About "the good life"? About the mystery of human suffering? If the quest for a spiritual life can shed some light on these all-important questions, the journey will be worth making.

2

Getting the Vision

I once saw a cartoon showing Moses holding the Ten Commandments. Around him several Hebrews were eyeballing the stone tablets, and one of them was saying, "O.K., O.K., but what's the bottom line?"

At this point I suspect that some of you might be thinking, "O.K., I would like to develop my spirituality, but tell me what I have to do." But that would be putting the cart before the horse. Spirituality, as I said before, includes both a way of seeing and a way of living. What I am saying now is that seeing comes first. We need to correct our vision before we can correct our behavior. Psychologists say, "Perception determines behavior"; common sense tells us the same thing. If I perceive people as basically hostile, I will conduct myself in their presence quite differently than if I perceive them as basically friendly. Father John Powell in *The Christian Vision* tells the story about the fellow who came home one night and thought he saw a 35-foot snake on his front lawn. As fear shot adrenalin through his system, he grabbed a garden hoe and began hacking away at the snake. When he figured it was dead, he went into the house, poured himself a drink and went to bed. Next morning he looked out on the front lawn and saw his garden hose cut into a dozen pieces.

If perceptions determine our behavior, what determines our perceptions? Generally speaking, the information at hand. If our friend in the preceding paragraph had had the benefit of adequate lighting, he would have perceived the "snake" as his friendly garden hose. Sometimes, however, we don't have adequate information available to us. Then we have to rely on habitual patterns of perception and attitudes which we learned in the past. Sometimes these at-

titudes are not even conscious. They are buried deep in our memories and they operate almost automatically:
- "Don't mix with those people; they're not our kind."
- "Keep your thoughts and feelings to yourself."
- "Treat others as you would want them to treat you."
- "Most people will show their best side if you give them a chance."

People who have learned a set of negative attitudes in earlier life tend to react to new situations by feeling anxious, threatened, suspicious and hostile. They are seldom relaxed and happy. One of the assumptions of contemporary psychotherapy is that people have problems because they are carrying around a set of distorted perceptions of reality. The therapist's task is to help the individual examine his or her habitual perceptions and attitudes in order to revise them in the direction of clearer reality.

Who Forms Our Visions?

While spiritual growth is not the same as psychotherapy, it does call for an examination of one's vision and perception. Am I seeing life in the way that God sees it, or not? Whose vision am I following? God's? Society's? My own? My peer group's? Through the prophet Haggai, God reminds us of how crucial it is that we learn to see with his vision. So much of our restlessness and emptiness come from clinging to our own illusions:

> Now thus says the LORD of hosts:
> Consider your ways!
> You have sown much, but have
>   brought in little;
>   you have eaten, but have not been
>   satisfied;
> You have drunk, but have not been
>   exhilarated;
>   have clothed yourselves, but have not
>   been warmed;
> And he who earned wages
>   earned them for a bag with holes
>   in it (Hg 1:5-6).

These are powerful images. We all know the feeling of having worked so hard and to have so little to show for it, of tasting so many of the good things of life but still not feeling fulfilled. Could it be that we have been mistaken, misled about the very meaning and purpose of life? Spirituality invites us to "examine our ways." Who shapes my vision? Whose values have I chosen to embody? Who has authority over my mind and over my choices? Some years ago *Redbook* magazine surveyed its readers with the question: "Where do you get your moral guidelines?" I was shocked to learn that only 17 percent answered "from my religion." Practically all the others gave one of two responses: "from my friends," or "from the media." Think of what that means: Most people are giving more authority over their lives to peers, TV stars and talk-show guests than they are to God. Is it any wonder that our nation is drifting on a moral collision course?

Christians have always claimed to have a different vision from that propounded by the society around them. I once heard a friend of mine, Father Michael Crosby, give a talk on "Praying the Our Father as a Subversive Activity." He pointed out that the early Christians were obedient and respectful of civil authority unless it clashed with the teachings of Jesus Christ. Then they were willing to risk persecution and rejection. They took seriously what Jesus said in the gospel: "No one can serve two masters. . . . You cannot give yourself to God and money" (Mt 6:24). Even when praying the Our Father these Christians were aware that they were making a choice of God over the Roman Empire. "Our Father who art in heaven"—not "our Emperor who art in Rome." Those Christians could not pray the Lord's Prayer unless they were willing to live out the consequences: "Vision determines behavior."

In his book *Call to Conversion* Jim Wallis reminds us of what St. Peter wrote to the first Christians: "Be ready to give an explanation to anyone who asks you for a reason for your hope" (1 Pt 3:15). He notes that Peter simply took it for granted that nonbelievers would notice something different about Christians and would be curious to know why they live the way they do. How come, Wallis says, nobody asks that kind of question any more? The answer is simple, he says: because modern Christians live pretty much the same as everyone else. There's nothing notably different about their lifestyle, so presumably there's nothing different about their vision or belief system.

From another viewpoint, sociologists of religion have noted a similar trend among contemporary American Catholics. For several generations Catholics in this country were largely an immigrant population. They were poor, they were uneducated, they suffered discrimination. Gradually, as they became educated and moved up the socioeconomic ladder, they became accepted and assimilated into the American mainstream. So much so, the surveys indicate, that Catholics are as likely as anyone else to be corporate executives, university professors, judges, managers and members of Congress. But they are also as likely as anyone else to be criminals, to cheat in their business practices, to be unfaithful to their spouses and neglectful of their families. The price for acceptance, it seems, has been loss of moral and spiritual identity.

The main reason for this erosion, I believe, is that we, without fully realizing it, have allowed our vision to be shaped by something other than the gospel of Jesus Christ. His gospel is in fierce competition with what I and others call "the cultural gospel." There is another set of values and standards around that is so all-pervasive that we barely recognize it, much less examine and challenge it. For purposes of illustration, let me line up these two gospels in order to compare their differences.

Gospel of Christ	*Cultural Gospel*
Blessed are the poor in spirit	Blessed are the rich and comfortable
Blessed are the meek	Blessed are the tough
Blessed are they who hunger and thirst for righteousness	Blessed are they whose every want is satisfied
Blessed are the merciful	Blessed are they who get even
Blessed are you when they insult you and persecute you	Blessed are you when they accept you and pamper you
Give, and it shall be given to you in good measure	Look out for yourself; nobody else will.
Take up [your] cross each day and follow me	Avoid pain and suffering at all costs
What profit would there be for one to gain the whole world and forfeit his life?	Success is the name of the game; you're a loser if you don't achieve it
All who take the sword will perish by the sword	The only way to peace is to have more and better weapons
Love the Lord your God with all your heart . . . and with all your mind	Go to church and keep up appearances, but don't be a religion freak

I don't think we realize deeply enough how much that cultural gospel affects us. It is in the very air we breathe. It finds expression in so many places: in advertising, in movies and television shows, in self-help books, even in public policies. We cannot even denounce the cultural gospel as false, because every one of its statements contains some truth. The difference between it and the gospel of Christ is more subtle. It is not so much that one is true and the other false, but that one is deep and the other shallow; one is long-range and the other is immediate; one is appealing and the other challenging. And it is deep in our human nature to prefer the quick-fix, the tangible and the pleasurable.

Faith and the Bible

Here we come to the reason why Christians need to be steeped in the Bible. We need an alternative to the cultural gospel. We want to know: What is God's vision of the good life?

Adult Catholics today often ask, "Why weren't we taught the Bible in our earlier formation?" The question comes out of a sense of inadequacy, almost an inferiority complex, because they find that their Protestant friends are so much more knowledgeable about scripture. Catholics sometimes feel they were cheated.

The feeling is understandable. Catholic spirituality a few generations ago did tend to downplay the importance of the Bible. We put our emphasis on knowing our catechism and our rituals. Our catechism, it was presumed, gave us the answers to the great questions of life. Most of us, for example, can still remember that very first catechism question: "Why are we in this world?" And the answer: "We are in this world to know God, to love him, and to serve him in this life, and to be happy with him forever in heaven." Bingo. It was a beautiful answer to a profound question. And you didn't have to go looking all over the Bible to find it. We knew that our church had a lot of truths to teach us, and it was our job to learn them. Our rituals, such as the Sign of the Cross, the Creed and the Mass, were ways of helping us to keep the truths alive in our minds and hearts.

That was one approach to spirituality, and it worked pretty well. We were accused of putting the church ahead of the Bible, but at least we avoided the pitfall of everybody interpreting the Bible the way he or she felt inspired to.

But that approach also had its weaknesses. For one thing, there was always the danger of knowing the doctrines only in our heads and never really letting them energize our hearts. We could become robot-like Christians, reciting the formulas from memory and keeping the rules, but not really alive, joyful and Spirit-filled. Moreover, by neglecting the Bible we lost touch with the great stories of men and women who struggled with God and with their faith. We learned the image of the all-perfect, triumphant God, but not the mysterious biblical God who gets tired and irritated and says he feels rejected like a jilted lover.

A lot has happened since the catechism days. For one thing, we rediscovered our own Catholic history and found that there is a long tradition of scripture reading in our church. The first Christian communities used to gather in homes to read the Hebrew scriptures and to recall the words and deeds of Jesus of Nazareth, whom they believed was the risen Lord of history. Indeed, that process eventually gave rise to the four gospels and some other books of the New Testament. Furthermore, we found that daily scripture reading was the practice of many Catholic Christians for generations.

Then, in 1943, Pope Pius XII wrote an encyclical letter encouraging Catholic biblical scholars to pursue their task with new vigor, in order to assist the faithful in better understanding and appreciating the word of God. This opened a whole new era of scripture study in the church and helped to set the stage for the Second Vatican Council. At the council itself, every session began with a ceremony of enthroning the scripture—carrying the Bible in procession by the assembled bishops. The bishops wanted to symbolize their desire to have all their deliberations guided by the word of God. And in its decree on Divine Revelation, the council declared that "all the preaching of the Church, indeed the whole Christian religion, should be nourished and ruled by Sacred Scripture" (n. 21).

Let's pause again and take stock. We have been saying that spirituality is a vision, a way of seeing reality. For spirituality to be Christian, it has to reflect God's vision of the good life, not just our own or society's. That vision is revealed first of all in the Bible, especially in the life and teachings of Jesus Christ. This means that if we want to develop a spirituality and grow in it, we need to be in touch with the scriptures.

Note that this is the very first time I'm talking about a specific *practice*. So far I've been describing spirituality in terms of attitude

PBAP P3/39

or vision. But now we have to get to the question: How do we acquire the vision? My answer: We listen to the word of God in scripture.

I realize that I may be going out on a limb here. I know that some men are not much into reading. Does that mean they cannot have a solid spirituality? I would not want to draw that conclusion. That's why I purposely used the word "listen" rather than "read" in the previous paragraph. It may be that some men can acquire spiritual vision by listening carefully to the scriptures at Mass or by listening to good preaching on the radio or television; however, I believe we have to read the word of God in order to be formed by it. Reading is a way of getting personally involved with the text. We need to wrestle with the word, just as Jacob wrestled with the angel. I'm talking, though, about a certain kind of reflective reading or "meditation," which I'll describe a little later.

First, there is one thing we need to be clear about. The Bible is not just about the past. It would be easy to dismiss it by saying, "That stuff all happened a long time ago. It has nothing to do with my life now." If that were true, the Bible would have stopped selling a long time ago. Why does it continue to outrank all other books in total sales? The answer can only be: because its stories and truths are timeless. It addresses the deepest questions of the heart: Who am I? What is the purpose of my life? Where is my center—the base from which all my decisions flow? Who is God? What is his plan for human happiness? Our minds are hungry for the truth. The Bible teaches us the truth about ourselves and about the world we live in. It teaches us how to become our best self.

The other conviction we need to have is that the Bible is not just a human word, but the word of God. We saw in the first chapter that God takes the initiative in communicating with us. He does that in a number of ways, but one of them is through the great themes of the scriptures. As we saw in the first chapter, God's initiative calls for response on our part. In this case, our response is to listen to God's word in order to acquire his vision of reality. Another word for this activity is *prayer*.

Faith and Prayer

Some Catholics, I believe, have grown up with a lot of experience of "saying prayers" but not much experience of "praying." They learned how to recite the Our Father, the Hail Mary, the Creed, the

Act of Contrition, meal prayers, maybe the rosary. I call these formula prayers, because they consist of set forms and words that somebody else composed for our use. They can be perfectly good forms of prayer. They put us in touch with the great truths of our faith and help us to put our thoughts and feelings into words. Praying the psalms is another good example of formula prayer. This kind of prayer is especially helpful when we are agitated or distracted and really need some vehicle or structure to lift our minds and hearts to God. The weakness of formula prayer is that it may not express our true attitudes and feelings. The words are not our own. We can say them with little or no thought or personal involvement. How, for example, can we pray "Thy will be done," when we are inwardly rebelling at the news that we've just lost our job? Or "I believe in the communion of saints," when we've just had our house vandalized by hoodlums?

This is why we need a more inclusive notion of prayer. I like to define prayer as "any act whereby we consciously attend to the presence of God within us or around us." The two key notions here are "presence of God" and "consciously attend." We saw in the first chapter that Christian spirituality is founded on the truth that God is continually inviting us into relationship with himself. We called that the first movement of spirituality. And we said that the second movement is our response to God's invitations. When we consciously attend to the presence of God, then, we are responding. We are completing the circle. We are praying. Formula prayer is one way but there are many others. We can talk to God in our own words. We can sing a song. We can quietly reflect on some word or truth that just struck us in a new way. We can simply remain in silent wonder at the Mystery that surrounds us. All are forms of prayer.

Another important truth about prayer is that God wants us to bring ourselves before him exactly as we are. No phoniness, no cover-ups, no need to launder our words. Here is where I have found the Old Testament so helpful. The Hebrew people felt free enough with God to be completely themselves. They could complain and carry on before the Lord with no fear of reprisals from him. Check out Psalm 73, for example. The believer is struggling with the problem, "Why do the good guys finish last?" He says:

> . . . I was envious of the arrogant
>   when I saw them prosper though they were
>   wicked.

For they are in no pain,
    their bodies are sound and sleek;
They are free from the burdens of mortals,
    and are not afflicted like the rest of
        men. . . .
Is it but in vain I have kept my heart clean,
    and washed my hands as an innocent man?
For I suffer affliction day after day,
    and chastisement with each new dawn (Ps
        73: 3-5: 15-14).

Doesn't that sound like us when we feel we've been cheated by life? We wonder why God allows some people to get away with all kinds of wrongdoing, while so many good people seem to suffer more than their share of life's hardships. The mental pain is especially acute when it is we ourselves or our loved ones who get hit. We wonder if it "pays" to be virtuous and God-centered. This is not the place to go into a theology of suffering. My only point now is that believers have always felt free to question God, to give voice to their feelings of weariness and even rebellion—precisely because they believed that God was a friend with whom they could be honest.

Even Moses, whom the Bible calls God's "intimate friend" (Ex 33:12), got exasperated with God on more than one occasion and told him so. One time, when the Israelites were getting tired of their daily ration of manna and wanted some good meat for a change, Moses lost his cool and had it out with the Lord:

"Why do you treat your servant so badly?" Moses asked the Lord. "Why are you so displeased with me that you burden me with all this people? Was it I who conceived them, or was it I who gave them birth . . . ? Where can I get meat to give to all this people? . . . I cannot carry all of them by myself, for they are too heavy for me. If this is the way you will deal with me, then please do me the favor of killing me at once, so that I need no longer face this distress" (Nm 11:11-15).

Doesn't that sound like you and me when we feel the people in our lives are demanding more than we can possibly give? And let's not miss the fact that the great Moses was expressing thoughts that psychiatrists today would call suicidal. He was definitely in the pits. The story has a happy ending, though, because God says, "O.K., O.K., I'll give you some people to help you" (see Nm 11:16-17).

My point here is simply that God wants us to be honest in our prayer. We don't have to put up a front for him. If we're heavy with discouragement, if we're smoldering with resentment, if we're feeling lustful, if we're lonely, if we want revenge—whatever our mental or emotional state—we can bring it all to prayer. God knows it all anyway. As the scripture says, "Nothing is concealed from him; all lies bare and exposed" to his eyes (Heb 4:13). But this divine knowledge is healing, not intimidating. The author continues: "So let us confidently approach the throne of grace to find mercy and favor and to find grace for timely help" (Heb 4:16).

Praying With Scripture

I would like now to describe a form of prayer called "praying with scripture." Again, I want to stress that this is but one form of prayer. Its special advantage, I think, is that it has the potential to combine scripture reading with personal, spontaneous prayer coming from our own depths. And it can help us to grow in our understanding of God's vision for human life and happiness.

In the first place, this kind of prayer is not something that we rush into. What we do immediately before prayer is very important. We spend a few minutes quieting ourselves down, relaxing and settling into a comfortable position. We recall that God is present to us in a personal way at this very moment.

Then I usually review the previous day. I recall the good things that happened and thank the Lord for each of them. If some things were painful or disappointing, I try to give them over to him. If I'm worried or upset about something, or struggling with a decision, I ask him to help me see it as he does. Then I ask him for the grace to listen now to his word in the scriptures.

Next I select a scripture passage for reading and reflection. There are different ways of doing this. If you have a daily missal (or if your parish bulletin lists the daily readings), you can use the scriptures for the Mass of the day. Or, you can take one of the gospels (or any other book of the Bible) and read a few verses each day. Usually five to ten verses are enough, but don't break up a complete story or unit.

I usually read the passage through once, just to get a "feel" for it as a whole. I note the words or phrases that strike me, or the general theme or point of the passage. Then I go over it slowly and reflectively, trying to see connections between these words of scripture and the things I've just been thinking about from my own life. The questions I always have in the back of my mind are: What truth is God trying to teach me here? How does that truth connect with my life? What response am I being called to make? And I listen carefully for "answers" to those questions. I don't really hear the voice of God speaking, but I pay very close attention to the thoughts, feelings and intuitions that come to me in the silence.

Sometimes there is no direct connection with the "stuff" of my life, but I just get a different or deeper insight into the ways of God or into life's larger questions. Usually, also, I will feel moved to praise God, to thank him for blessings ("I had a terrible dream last night and I want to thank you that it was only a dream!"), to ask him for what I and others need. Sometimes I will ask him questions: What does this phrase in the scripture mean? How do you want me to deal with so-and-so? Why isn't that project of mine going anywhere? Sometimes I receive an answer, sometimes I don't. Then I figure God needs some more time to think about it, and I come back to pester him the next day. Finally, I usually end by making some specific requests for myself and others, and end with the Our Father or some other formula prayer.

I think you can see that the assumption I'm making is that prayer is simply an act of communication between friends. I will say more about the basis for our friendship with God in the next chapter. My point now is that we can be as free and open with God in prayer as we are with any other friend. Moreover, if we want to strengthen a relationship with someone, the best and most direct way to do so is by spending time with that person.

This way of praying with scripture is sometimes called meditation. I would like to share with you now an example of this kind of prayer, taken from my own experience. A few years ago I made a directed retreat at a time when I was coming off of some painful experiences and feeling sorry for myself. The first day I met with my director he asked me to pray over Isaiah 55:1-11. As I did, I made notes of my reflections; I share them with you as an example of praying with scripture.

An Example of Prayer

The first thing I notice is how often God says "come" and "listen." How passionately God pursues us—and not because he needs

us, but because he wants our happiness so strongly. He knows how
easily we look somewhere else for it. . . .

vs. 1:
> All you who are thirsty,
> > come to the water!
> You who have no money,
> > come, receive grain and eat.
> Come, without paying and without cost,
> > drink wine and milk!"

I've certainly come here "thirsty." I was not enthused about coming;
it seemed like one more "should" in my life. But now that I'm here, I
realize how thirsty I am. I can hardly get enough of the scriptures—
and of solitude. "Come, without paying and without cost." It struck
me what a luxury this retreat is. How many people can take eight
days out of their life to do nothing but take stock of their life in the
light of God's word? Again I feel gratitude. . . .

vs. 2:
> Why spend your money for what is
> > not bread;
> your wages for what fails to satisfy?

Right on! Sunday I spent $5.50 to play golf—and all it did was de-
press me! That's only a symbol of what I keep doing to myself over
and over. It's not so much the money as the time and the false expectations: This or that will satisfy me—but it never does.
This tells me what will:

vs. 2-3:
> Heed me, and you shall eat well. . . .
> Come to me heedfully,
> > listen, that you may have life.

This leads me to my prayer practices. Lord, you know I've been quite
faithful and regular in devoting time to prayer, but I think it's become another "should." I don't come to you "heedfully" or joyfully,
really expecting to be filled. I need to reflect more on this: How can I
come to prayer with a more receptive attitude?

vs. 6:
> Seek the Lord while he may be found;
> > call him while he is near.

It strikes me as odd, Lord: Can't you always be "found"? Aren't you always "near"? What's the urgency? Maybe it has something to do with passion. If you are passionate in seeking me, shouldn't my response be similar? If I don't seek you now, while you are near; if I seek you only half-heartedly or as an also-ran, am I not in danger of losing you? Or at least, making you remote or harmless? . . . In any case, I know how laid-back I can become about seeking you, Lord, and how I can spend passion on "what fails to satisfy."

vs. 8-9:
> For my thoughts are not your thoughts,
> > nor are your ways my ways, says the LORD.
> As high as the heavens are above the earth,
> > so high are my ways above your ways,
> > and my thoughts above your thoughts.

Verse 7 says that the scoundrel must forsake his way and the wicked man his thoughts. But the text implies that all of us need to submit our thoughts and ways to God's. It's strange, but I find more comfort than challenge in that. Lord, I'm glad my thoughts and ways are not the last word, the final measure of reality. The challenge is to keep measuring them against yours. But the comfort is that even when my perception of something is negative, or I meet with apparent failure, it may not be so in your eyes. Your ways are above mine. You can see farther and better. Once again, I'm called to do what I honestly think best, and leave the outcome to you.

vs. 10-11:
> For just as from the heavens
> > the rain and snow come down
> And do not return there
> > till they have watered the earth,
> > making it fertile and fruitful . . .
> So shall my word be
> > that goes forth from my mouth;
> It shall not return to me void,
> > but shall do my will,
> > achieving the end for which I sent it.

The ancients thought of life as a repetitive cycle going nowhere. This is a totally different vision: God's word breaks in and has an impact. I need to hold on to this truth, Lord. I can get very pessimistic and cynical about the state of the world and the church—it seems like the gospel doesn't have a chance. I have to believe that your word "shall not return to you void, but shall do your will." I never know when and how this is going to happen. So often I've been amazed that people were touched by what I thought was a trite, obvious statement I had made—or by something I didn't even remember saying. Your word, Lord, is both weak and powerful. My job is to give it every chance to be heard. Again I'm reminded of Cardinal Newman's prayer: "God does nothing in vain. He knows what he is about. . . . Therefore I will trust him."

Please don't get the idea that things flow this neatly every time I sit down to pray! Far from it. Most of the time my thoughts and prayers are a jumbled mess. But that need not discourage us. God really does accept us wherever we are at the time. We certainly will not come to new truths or insights each time. Sometimes we will just receive a deeper understanding or appreciation of what we already believe. But that too is a valuable gift. And sometimes the only response God wants of us is adoration, gratitude, or a deeper desire to know his will. That's enough.

Finally, let me say something about the time and place for prayer. For myself, I find that I need to take some special time for prayer practically every day. So I try to build it into my day, pretty much at the same time. If I don't pray regularly, I notice two things happening to me: One, I get irritable and grouchy; and two, I tend to be shallow in my approach to people and to problems. The reason just has to be that I am losing clear vision. I am not seeing with God's eyes or moving with his divine energy. And more and more men I talk to are telling me the same thing. So they are trying to structure daily prayer and scripture reading into their lives. Some are doing it with their wives or with a group. Others are doing it on their lunch break. They are carving out time and space to nourish their relationship with the Lord. Remember, too, even if your mind is all cluttered with distractions, at least your body is there. You are praying with your body. You are telling God that at least you want to pray, and you are giving that time and energy to him. Just remaining humbly in his presence is itself an act of prayer.

We started this chapter by pointing out how strongly our perceptions influence our behavior. That helped us to see how important it is for our spiritual life that we perceive reality clearly and according to God's vision. Because our society feeds us so many distorted images and downright false values, we need regular contact with God's word in scripture in order to maintain a clear spiritual vision. This led us to a discussion of prayer, its various forms and its place in the life of a Christian. Finally, we took a more extended look at one particular prayer form, praying with scripture.

Now we want to focus our spiritual vision on what is perhaps the most crucial and vulnerable area of our lives: our self-image.

3

Who Am I?

One of our priests who has conducted a lot of retreats for teens and young adults recently told me about a 20-year-old fellow who said to him, "The world is a stinking mess. That's why I get 'bombed' every night."

We adults can easily see through his rationalization. "Why doesn't he get out of his stupor and start doing something constructive for the world?" we say. Absolutely correct. But maybe this young man is also speaking for a good number of males who feel very unsure about their ability to cope with life as it is. After all, it is not easy to be a male in contemporary America. Just think of the composite image of maleness portrayed for us in the media: The ideal man is college-educated, has the perfect body of an athlete, is an irresistible sex partner as well as a tender lover, is tough and competitive on the job (but smart enough to stay out of trouble and not make waves), owns a nice home and a classy car, is sophisticated in the ways of the world and knows just what to wear on all occasions.

Who can live up to that? Most men that I know are average-looking, are struggling to hold on to rather unglamorous jobs, have to work hard at their marriages and worry about their kids far more than about their clothes. It is all too easy for them to judge themselves as having failed to live up to the cultural ideal. If they are too forceful and dominant in personal relationships, they are accused of being macho; if they are too passive and easygoing, they are called "wimps."

I don't think we always appreciate how profoundly the changes in society have affected us. I recently heard an enlightening set of tapes by Father Richard Rohr entitled, "A Man's Approach to God." He quoted a social scientist who said, "Since the Industrial Revolution what has been most destroyed is the father-son relationship." Be-

fore that, Father Rohr commented, boys grew up in immediate relationship with their fathers: They worked alongside them on the farm
or in the family business. The son had a domain and an identity. He
knew who he was and he knew he was accepted.

Since then, fathers go away to work in factories and offices. This
has left a vacuum in the sons "into which many demons have en-
tered" (see Lk 8:30), as Father Rohr says: the demons of mistrust of
the masculine, of authority and of sexuality. He tells about the nun
who was working in prison ministry. Before Mother's Day nearly all
the prisoners asked her to buy cards for them so they could send them
to their mothers. So the next month, when it got close to Father's
Day, the nun went out and bought a whole box of cards so she
wouldn't have to keep going out for a couple at a time. To her surprise and dismay, not one prisoner asked for a Father's Day card.
These were men who, for whatever reason, have felt robbed of the
positive masculine energy found in good father-son relationships and
have taken out their anger on society. I am not excusing them, nor
am I blaming "society" for whatever is wrong with American males.
I am only saying there are realities here that we need to understand if
we are going to develop a healthy spirituality.

Another reality, I believe, is that contemporary American society is
highly competitive. I remember enrolling some years ago in a course in
cultural anthropology. One of the first articles we had to read was about
the Zuni Indians in the Southwest. The author began by saying,
"Among the Zunis, a child is accepted merely by being born; he doesn't
have to prove anything." That statement made such an impression on
me that I never forgot it. What a contrast, I thought, with our own culture. We are forever feeling the need to prove ourselves. Competition is
the name of the game. We are forever comparing and being compared
with others, trying to reassure ourselves that we come off better—
whether it's our toys, our clothes, our bug collection, or our baby sister.
As we get older, the game doesn't change but the stakes get higher; now
we compare grades, athletic skills, exploits and friends. Still later, we
adults compare schools attended, degrees achieved, positions held,
tastes cultivated and possessions owned.

A certain amount of competition is just plain human and even
fun. It certainly inspires progress and improvement. What I am concerned about here is the negative fallout. Competitiveness can come
to dominate all other values, including religion. I once saw an ad for

tailor-made suits featuring a handsome young man who was saying: "Being perfectly well-dressed gives a feeling of tranquillity that religion is powerless to bestow." Really now?

What about those who can't keep up with the competition? Are they merely the certain percentage of casualties who have to be factored into any social system? Are they any less valuable as human beings because they lost? And what about those who do manage to keep up? What price are they paying in terms of stress-related illnesses, alcohol and drug abuse, strained marriages, divorces, sheer lack of time and energy for the things of the Spirit? A popular song put it into one sad line: "I ran so fast that time and youth ran out, I never stopped to think what life was all about."

My point here is that these images of masculinity and this strong stress on competition can generate an unhealthy anxiety and feeling of inadequacy in us males. As we said in the previous chapter, our culture's value messages are so pervasive and persistent that it is not easy to resist them. They can come to dominate our consciousness. Then we are in danger of letting ourselves be named and judged and valued by the standards of society instead of by the word of God. And if we see ourselves falling short of the cultural ideal, we may go through life with a gnawing sense of inferiority, a diminished sense of self-worth that saps our vitality.

How Does God See Us?

This brings us back to the importance of a correct "vision," as we discussed in the last chapter. The question now is: If contemporary society's vision of the real man is inadequate because it is based too much on competitiveness and macho domination, what is the alternative? What is God's answer to the question: "Who am I?"

Here we need to pick our way carefully through the Bible. It is so easy to come up with an oversimplified or one-sided answer. If we read the Bible selectively, we can conclude either that we are walking saints or hardened sinners. The truth is more like the classic "good news-bad news." Let's take the bad news first.

The scriptures go to great lengths to show that human beings are finite creatures who are not to claim equality with God. The so-called Wisdom books of the Old Testament are particularly eloquent about this. It says in the book of Job, for example:

But whence can wisdom be obtained,
and where is the place of understanding?
Man knows nothing to equal it,
    nor is it to be had in the land
        of the living. . . .
God knows the way to it;
    it is he who is familiar with
        its place (Job 28:12, 13, 23).

Later, after Job and his friends have been arguing about the
ways of God for 37 chapters, God breaks in and sets them all straight

Who is this that obscures divine
    plans with words of ignorance?
Gird up your loins now, like a man;
    I will question you, and you tell
        me the answers!
Where were you when I founded the earth?
Tell me, if you have understanding. . . .
Then Job answered the Lord and said:
Behold, I am of little account;
    what can I answer you?
I put my hand over my mouth (Jb 38: 2-4; 40:3-4).

Not only are human beings limited in what they can understand
and what they can achieve; they have a deep-seated tendency to
make choices that are contrary to God's purposes and ultimately to
their own happiness. This is stated powerfully in Jeremiah:

Thus says the Lord:
What fault did your fathers find
    in me that they withdrew from me,
Went after empty idols,
    and became empty themselves? . . .
Be amazed at this, O heavens,
    and shudder with sheer horror,
        says the Lord.
Two evils have my people done:
    they have forsaken me, the source
        of living waters;
They have dug themselves cisterns,
    broken cisterns, that hold no
        water (Jer 2:5, 12-13).

Anyone who is honest about it has no difficulty recognizing that there is some basic flaw in our human nature. The church has called it "original sin." It simply means that every one of us has something deep inside us that wants to put our own self-interest above every other consideration. We all know from experience exactly what St. Paul means when he says, "Even though I want to do what is right, a law that leads to wrongdoing is always ready at hand. My inner self agrees with the law of God; but I see in my body's members another law at war with the law of my mind" (Rom 7:21-22). I know this is me. I do get enthused about wanting to give my very best for God and for his people. But then I'll turn around and do something nasty, petty, or downright selfish—and I feel like an idiot. I've come to realize, though, that this does not make me a bad person. All it means is that I am weak and in need of help from a source outside of myself.

Human Dignity

Which brings us to the good news. The Bible dwells more insistently on human dignity than on human sinfulness. Psalm 8, for example, is a beautiful meditation on the dignity of men and women whom God created "in his own image and likeness" (see Gn 1:27):

> O LORD, our LORD,
> how glorious is your name over all
> the earth! . . .
> What is man that you should be
> mindful of him;
> or the son of man that you should
> care for him?
> You have made him little less than
> the angels,
> and crowned him with glory and
> honor (Ps 8:2, 5-6).

A couple of years ago I was waiting for my appointment in the dentist's office. To distract myself from the ordeal ahead, I picked up a copy of the *National Geographic*. The feature article was on the latest theory on the origin of the universe, a subject which always fascinates me. I don't remember all the details, but the scientists hypothesize that "in the beginning" was a large ball of gases and particles of matter. The scientists don't try to explain where the large ball came from, but anyway they think that it began to condense into a smaller and heavier mass, until it was about the size of an orange. At some point, one of two things was most likely to occur. Either the ball would continue to condense until it became so heavy that it would simply become another "black hole" in space. Or, it would start to expand so rapidly that it would disintegrate and burn out. What actually happened, according to the theory, is that the ball expanded at exactly the right speed and temperature, resulting in the formation of our solar system and countless other galaxies.

Now, the probability of such a thing happening by chance alone, according to the mathematicians involved, was 10^{-32}. Written out, it would look like this: .00000000000000000000 000000000001. When you realize that "one chance in a million" looks like this: .0000001, you understand how incredibly slight the chances are. To put it even more vividly, the author said it would be like throwing an imaginary dart from the earth to the nearest star in our galaxy and hitting a bulls-eye one inch in diameter! At that point I put the magazine down and felt a profound sense of awe. Suddenly "the creation of the universe by God" was more than a doctrine or a group of words. It was an undeniable truth, an incomparably beautiful mystery.

From there my mind was led easily to the beginning of Paul's letter to the Ephesians: "Blessed be the God and Father of our Lord Jesus Christ, who has blessed us in Christ with every spiritual blessing in the heavens, as he chose us in him, before the foundation of the world . . ." (Eph 1:3-4). Think of it: Even before the ball of gases was formed, God had you and me in his mind and heart. Once again, "the dignity of the human person" becomes much more than an abstract truth. It has profound implications for the way we regard human life—the unborn infant, the handicapped, the elderly, the poor and disadvantaged. And it has power to heal our own self-doubts and anxieties about our self-worth. Society's ways of valuing us and measuring us become downright meaningless. Pope John Paul II put it so well in one of his addresses: "Before God every human being is unique and unrepeatable—someone chosen by God from all eternity, someone loved and called by his or her own name."

Positive Images

The scriptures are filled with positive images of the human personality. It seems as though God was aware of how much trouble we would have in accepting ourselves, so he went out of his way to affirm us in our self-worth:

> But now, thus says the LORD,
> who created . . . and formed you . . . :
> Fear not, for I have redeemed you;
> I have called you by name; you are mine.
> When you pass through the water, I will be with you;
> in the rivers you shall not drown.
> When you walk through fire, you shall not be burned;
> the flames will not consume you. . . .
> Because you are precious in my eyes
> and glorious, and because I love you . . .
> (Is 43:1-2, 4).

In the New Testament, Jesus keeps bringing his disciples back to the basic truth that their self-worth does not depend so much on their accomplishments as on their identity as his disciples and beloved sons of the Father. When he sent them out the first time to proclaim the good news in his name, they came back full of enthusiasm over all they had been able to accomplish. He was happy for them, but then he reminded them, "Do not rejoice so much in the fact that the devils are subject to you as that your names are inscribed in heaven" (Lk 10:20). That is, even more than their accomplishments is the fact that their name and their person is held in reverence by the Father. There is no reason for them to be afraid (Mt. 10:19). The Father loves them and dwells within them (Jn 14:23). He will send the Holy Spirit to be their friend and guide on life's journey (Jn 14:16).

We males are particularly prone to measure ourselves by our achievements. Maybe that's one reason why the church developed the practice of infant baptism. For a while I went through a stage when I thought it would be good to postpone baptism until the child is able to make a free choice to be a Christian. But as I thought about it, I began to realize more clearly that infant baptism is a great way to challenge society's whole system of valuing people on the basis of performance. Here is this tiny infant (the very word "infans" in Latin means "unable to speak") who has absolutely no accomplishments to its credit; yet the family, the church and God himself are all telling it how blest and beautifully welcome it is. "Little baby," we say, "as time goes on we will expect more of you; there will be tasks to perform and roles to be filled. But right now we commit ourselves to keep giving you one great positive

message: You are great, you are precious, you are holy—just because
you are a child of God and one of our human family."

I'm fully aware that not all children are lucky enough to have
grown up in that kind of affirming environment. Too often they receive
very negative messages about how inadequate they are and how God
can't possibly be pleased with them. For some, this can result in psychological damage in the form of chronic low self-esteem. Sometimes the
damage can be repaired through good counseling or psychotherapy.
Other people have been restored to wholeness by healing prayer and the
power of the sacraments. In any case, a stressful childhood need not be a
permanent barrier to God's transforming grace.

So, then, the biblical vision of the human person is not black and
white. We are both gifted and limited, exalted and humbled, sinful yet
redeemed. This truth has a couple of important implications for our
spiritual life. For one thing, it sheds light on the much-misunderstood
Christian virtue of humility. I'm afraid the notion of humility has taken
a beating in recent years. Sometimes it has been badly used to justify a
poor self-image. That is, people were taught to despise themselves so
they wouldn't get trapped in pride or self-love.

But the truth is, not only does God not forbid us to love ourselves,
he even commands us to do so: "You shall love your neighbor *as yourself.*" To hear self-love proclaimed as a virtuous possibility instead of a
sin could be truly liberating for some Christians. In the past we have not
emphasized enough the sacredness of our personality. If we have been
created in the image of God, as the Bible insists, then we have no right to
despise God's handiwork.

Too often the attitude of self-depreciation has been identified with
humility and self-esteem has been confused with the sin of pride. In this
connection, it is refreshing to recall that St. Thomas Aquinas once defined humility as "the reasonable pursuit of one's own excellence." We
could hardly find a more psychologically healthy statement. It asserts
that we do have a God-given excellence and that we are called to develop it in accordance with reason. Pride, then, would be the unreasonable pursuit of our excellence, any kind of inordinate striving that would
do violence to others or fly in the face of our own limitations.

The Reality of Sin

The other connection with spirituality has to do with the issue of
sin in our lives. Christian spiritual writers have always pointed out

the need for a healthy sense of sin in one who is trying to grow in relationship with God. This does not mean a morbid preoccupation, a scrupulous examination of all our actions to see where we have deviated or fallen short. Rather, it is an honest awareness and acknowledgment of our wrong moral choices and attitudes. It is often said nowadays that contemporary Catholics have lost a healthy sense of sin. Whereas in the past we may have been too sin-centered and guilt-ridden in our spiritual lives, today we seem to be swinging too far in the opposite direction. It is no secret that Catholics are staying away from the sacrament of reconciliation. An article in *U.S. Catholic* recently discussed "Ten Reasons Why Catholics Have Stopped Going to Confession." One of the reasons given was that they "don't consider sin as being prevalent in their lives as they once did."

Cultural forces have certainly been working behind the scenes. The stress on personal freedom and individual self-expression has made many people reluctant to see any wrongdoing in their actions. Contemporary novels, films, television programs and talk-shows all combine to give the impression that what used to be considered wrong is now acceptable—if for no other reason than that it is so commonplace. As one 16-year-old is supposed to have said in dismay, "I'm still a virgin—isn't it pathetic!" In an address to the 1985 convention of the American Psychological Association, Carol Tavris told the audience that "the seven capital sins in today's culture have acquired a certain respectability." She went on to suggest that pride is now hailed as "self-esteem," covetousness has become "upward mobility," envy is seen as "acquiring a competitive edge," lust has been transformed into "liberated sexuality," anger has been upgraded to "assertiveness," and sloth has been renamed "stress management"! Only gluttony, says Tavris, is still regarded as unacceptable, if not sinful.

My own Christian instinct leads me to denounce the cultural drift toward the denial of sin and the glamorizing of irresponsible behavior. But I also see some positive features in the new self-understanding that many Catholics are coming to. They are gaining a deeper appreciation of what it means to be redeemed by Christ, to be forgiven and accepted regardless of their mistakes. They do not want to go back to the old sin-centered spirituality that made them fearful and guilt-ridden.

But what would a "healthy sense of sin" look like? Basically, it would be an honest recognition that I have some deep-lying tendencies toward self-indulgence that are opposed to God's plan for my own and others' happiness; and furthermore, that I sometimes allow those tendencies to break out in the form of wrongful choices and actions. At the same time, this awareness does not depress me, because I know that God accepts me and forgives my sins.

For some reason (which probably has a lot to do with male ego), many men have a hard time developing this healthy sense of sin. Their instinctual reaction is "Not me!" They seem unable to accept the simple fact that they are human and have some weaknesses. Their whole cultural conditioning suggests that to be a man means to be strong, to be successful, to be in control. There is little or no room for human error, for mistakes or sins. Can you imagine the burden these men are carrying? To defend their vulnerable ego against any negative awareness, they rely on their two favorite mechanisms: denial and blaming. We have all known men who continue to drink themselves deeper into the grip of alcoholism while protesting, "I don't have a problem; I can stop any time!" Others somehow cram the problem behavior into a separate compartment of their mind, like the man who is carrying on an extra-marital affair while he continues to receive Communion every Sunday.

When denial doesn't work, the other easy defense is projection or blaming. In the days when I used to do a lot of marriage counseling, a typical scenario was this: The wife would come in and pour our her story of pain, tension and stress in the marriage. When I asked if the husband would also come for counseling, she would often say, "I asked him to come, but he says we should be able to solve our problems ourselves" (another typical macho idea). After a while I learned not to take the wife's statement as gospel; I would check it out by contacting the husband myself and inviting him to come in and give his side of the picture. Sometimes he would; but more often I would get a reply like, "Yeah? Well, her problem is that she listens to all those girlfriends of hers and they fill her head with garbage. She'd be happy if she got rid of them!"

You know, it takes a whole lot more psychic energy to deny and cover up our problems than it does to admit and deal with them. It is so much easier to sit down with another human being and say, "I need help. Where do I start?" For many an alcoholic, life literally began again when they took the first two steps of the A.A. program:

"We admitted that we were powerless over alcohol, that our lives had become unmanageable. And we believed that a Higher Power could restore us to sanity." St. Peter's spiritual conversion began when he knelt down at Jesus' feet in the fishing boat and cried out, "Depart from me, Lord, for I am a sinful man" (Lk 5:8). And Paul's began when he looked up into the blinding light and said to the risen Christ, "What shall I do, sir?" (Acts 22:10).

It is so important to realize that God regards this human nature of ours with both reverence and compassion. He does set high standards for us. What would we think of a God who expected little or nothing of those he has formed in his own image? On the other hand, God does not require a flawless performance. He knows our frailty, our limits, our tendency to doubt and waver and grasp at the illusions that dazzle us. When we fail, he is ready to forgive us. In that mysterious vision on Mount Sinai, Moses saw God passing before him and he cried out, "The LORD, the LORD, a merciful and gracious God!" (Ex 34:6). And the Psalmist prays,

> Bless the LORD, O my soul,
> > and forget not all his benefits;
> He pardons all your iniquities,
> > he heals all your ills (Ps 103:2-3).

Reconciliation and Healing

Jesus Christ in his wisdom has given us two sacraments to help us deal with the sinful and wounded side of our nature: reconciliation and the Eucharist. Here I don't want to go into all the reasons why reconciliation can be a psychologically healthy experience. I will confine myself to the question I hear many Catholics asking today: "Why can't I just confess my sins to God rather than having to go to the priest?" For me, there is only one good answer to that question: because that is not the way Christ set up the sacrament. He certainly could have. He might have said, for example, "When you know you are sorry for your sins, speak them in your heart and ask God's forgiveness." Or, "speak them to the stars above and ask God's forgiveness." But he didn't say that. What he said to the apostles was, "Receive the Holy Spirit. If *you* forgive people's sins, they are forgiven . . ." (Jn 20:23 emphasis mine). If the apostles and their successors are to know when and how to forgive sins, they need to know what it is that people are sorry for; and that means some kind of "confession" on the human level.

My own belief is that this direction of Jesus springs from profound wisdom and understanding of human nature. Most of us have a real need to tell our failings to another human being in order to feel "cleansed" and forgiven. Generations of bartenders, psychotherapists and advice columnists can testify to this. The truth is, though, none of these can give assurance of forgiveness. At most they can say, "I understand your behavior and I accept you in your humanness. I can even give you a 'penance' in the form of a fee. But if you want assurance that you are forgiven by God, you'd better go to your priest or minister."

But I think there is an even deeper reason why Jesus asks us to confess our sins to another human being. It is consistent with the whole sacramental system. That is, every one of the sacraments claims to "do" more than appears outwardly. Each one requires a leap of faith. Can the little water of baptism or oil of confirmation really work such a profound transformation in the very identity of a person—child of the Father, disciple of Jesus, dwelling place of the Spirit? Can a little bread and wine really contain the body and blood of Jesus Christ? And, in reconciliation, can the prayer of absolution spoken by the priest—himself a sinful human being—really speak the forgiveness and mercy of God? Catholics instinctively realize that the sacraments are awesome gestures, though they may not be able to explain them logically.

Lately I have been telling our retreat groups something else I believe about reconciliation. That is, even though we may not have serious sins to confess, it is good for our spiritual growth to celebrate reconciliation several times a year. I think we need to do this in order to remain honest and humble about who we are. We are not flawless, self-sufficient super-beings. We are fragile, forgetful, self-serving human beings who often play Trivial Pursuit with our lives. At the same time, we are the redeemed, baptized, beloved sons and daughters of the Father who is always ready to pour out his love and mercy upon us. Reconciliation helps us to maintain our Christian identity.

Today I hope we are beyond the anxiety of having to remember each and every one of our sins, or the routine laundry list: "I forgot my meal prayers; I cursed and swore; I had bad thoughts. . . ."

Today we realize it is far more helpful to bring to the Lord some of the basic attitudes or patterns that block our spiritual growth. For instance, when a man confesses, "Father, I see in myself a streak of laziness. It shows up in the fact that I keep putting off chores my wife asks me to do, and I get irritated with my kids when they want just a little attention and interest from me." Or, "I'm seeing a pattern in myself of always needing to be right. I over-react with anger when someone, especially in my family, questions one of my ideas or actions." As I tell the retreatants, "If you don't know what your sinful attitudes or patterns are, ask your wife—or your kids!" When we bring these tendencies before the Lord in the sacrament, he is able to touch them with his healing power and to gradually free us from their domination.

Eucharist and Healing

The other sacrament that heals our wounded self is the Eucharist. I do not want to go into a whole theology of the Eucharist here. I see something happening, though, that concerns me. Since Vatican II we have worked very hard at improving our eucharistic liturgy. We have brought priest and people closer together physically. We have increased participation of the people in praying, singing and performing liturgical ministries. We have developed a treasury of music in an incredibly short span of years. We have found creative ways to make our Mass more dynamic and meaningful. More Catholics than ever before are receiving communion at every Mass they attend. But there is a real danger, as well as much blessing, in all this. We can become so preoccupied with "doing the liturgy well" that we miss the real purpose of liturgy: worship of God and union with him. And our almost automatic participation in communion can become a routine action with little impact on our spiritual life.

One of the problems, of course, is that too many Catholics still attend Sunday Mass only out of a sense of obligation. They expect little and they receive little. But there are many others who attend with at least a vague hope that they will be touched, uplifted, and find a bit of faith and courage to help them through another week. These are the people I want to speak to in this section.

I once read a marvelous booklet by Father Eugene Walsh entitled *The Ministry of the Celebrating Community*. It left a deep impression on me and gave me some helpful ideas on how to be a better presider at the Eucharist. But he was really writing for the whole congregation assembled at Mass. He began by asking: What do we hope will happen at the liturgy? What is the real purpose of gathering for the Eucharist? His answer: to create for *everyone* the possibility of *an experience of God*. That really struck me. Not a word about obligation or mortal sin. No, we come to the Mass for a profoundly positive reason: to experience the presence of God, to "taste and see the goodness of the Lord" (Ps 34). That brings us back to the first chapter of this book, where we defined spirituality as the ongoing endeavor to grow in our relationship with God. Father Walsh reminds us that there are two natural and strong driving forces always at work between God and ourselves: first, the fact that God is always reaching out and inviting us to share in his love; and second, each of us, at some level, is desperately searching for fulfillment in life. So, the purpose of liturgy is to recognize and celebrate the presence of God giving hope and meaning to our lives. And we do that, not just by ourselves, but in communion with Christ and with our brothers and sisters.

Merely going through the ritual, however, is not enough to create the experience of God. In the past we more or less "trained" our Catholic people to be passive spectators at Mass, expecting something to be done to or for them, rather than helping them understand that they are called to be active participants. Moreover, we created an artificial distinction between priest and congregation, instead of creating the sense that together we form one celebrating community.

For Father Walsh, one of the key ways of increasing participation in the Mass is the simple notion of "paying attention." In the first place, we pay attention to one another. We cannot really worship with strangers, as though we just happened to be together in a movie theater. We somehow need to give the people around us the message, "Welcome! I'm really glad you're here." Lately I've had so many Catholics tell me about family members or friends who have left the church and joined fundamentalist churches. I myself am meeting an increasing number of former Catholics who have taken that route. So I've made it a point to ask them, "What are you finding there that you didn't find in the Catholic church?" Inevitably, the first answer is: "We really feel welcome. The other people take an interest in us. In the Catholic church everyone kept to themselves and it was so impersonal." That always saddens me. It would take so little to spend a few moments before or after Sunday Mass to greet the people around us, introduce ourselves if necessary and build a sense that we are worshiping God together as a community, a family.

Second, we need to pay attention to what the other members (especially the priest, readers, music directors) are doing and asking us to do with them. Of course, if their leadership is poor, it makes it harder for us to have a good experience of God. But *nothing* will happen if we do not even pay attention to their words and gestures. Did you ever really try paying attention to the readings, for example? Or to the words of the songs? If you do, you will be surprised how some word or phrase or idea will strike a note within you and give you something to think about all week long. Or, did you ever try really listening to the words of the Eucharistic Prayer? You will notice how the church "thinks big" when it prays: that all of us may be filled with the Holy Spirit; that we will come to form one body and one spirit; that divisions and barriers may be broken down; that peace and reconciliation will take place in our families and between nations.

Thirdly, Father Walsh says, we need to pay attention to what is going on inside of ourselves. How is God revealing himself to you? What does he want you to see? How are you being encouraged, strengthened, nourished? How are you being challenged? Can you see that disagreeable fellow at work in a new light? Can you surrender your anxieties to the Lord this week? As you approach the moment of communion, what are you hoping to receive from the Lord Jesus? Can you let your outstretched hand or tongue symbolize your profound need for him in your life?

I believe that this three-fold paying attention is a powerful way to increase our conscious participation in the Mass and prevent it from becoming the dull, routine experience many Catholics complain about. We Catholics have always believed that the Eucharist is the privileged place of our meeting with God. But we need to claim that heritage and personalize it for ourselves.

We began this chapter by asking the question: Who am I? We saw how easily we can allow the society around us to give us shallow, inadequate answers to that question, and that this is the source of much of our self-doubt and insecurity. We said that the full answer comes only from believing the word of God revealed to us in the Bible: We are both sinful and holy, wounded and redeemed, saved and struggling. We are called to believe that our deepest self is good, precious and positive; that God has breathed into our human nature a spark of his own divine life; indeed, we share that very life of God through our baptism in Christ Jesus. Finally, Christ has given us the sacraments of reconciliation and Eucharist to heal us of our sinful tendencies and to enable us to become our best and truest self. Now we want to see what implications this wonderful good news might have for our total lives—our jobs, our relationships and our problems.

4

The World of Work and Leisure

Most men in our society will spend at least one-half of their waking hours at their job. That's a big investment of time and energy. Unfortunately, most Christian men that I know don't think their job has anything to do with their spiritual life. More unfortunately, what they hear in church on Sundays does little to correct that misunderstanding.

Pope Paul VI once said that "one of the greatest evils of our time is the separation of religion from the rest of life." He was talking about the tendency to divide our lives into separate compartments: in particular, to confine the practice of our faith only to times of prayer and worship. How else can we explain the behavior of some Catholics, for example, who rush out of church right after communion and curse the guy who cuts in ahead of them at the parking lot exit! Or, more seriously, the reputedly devout Catholic who thinks nothing of taking bribes and kickbacks because "that's the way the business world operates."

Most people, I believe, want to live holistically, to "have it all together." A man who is unhappy or overly stressed at work is not likely to be pleasant at home or peaceful in his relationship with God. A couple of years ago a colleague of mine and I were asked by the diocese to conduct a retreat on "Faith and the Workplace" for business and professional people. It was an inspiration for me to listen to men and women who were struggling mightily to divide their time between jobs, their families and their commitments to service in the church. The other thing that struck me was the frequency with which they expressed a desire for a spirituality or a faith-vision that could pull their lives together. Recalling that retreat experience was another incentive for me to write this book. In this chapter I will take a look at work and leisure in connection with spirituality; in the next chapter, I want to discuss the connection between spirituality and family life.

Work and Human Personality

There is no question that a man's work is closely tied to his total reality as a person. In our American culture, at least, we even tend to define ourselves in terms of our jobs. When meeting new people, for example, the first question after exchanging names is generally, "What kind of work do you do?" And, whether we intend to or not, the answer to that question prompts within us all sorts of judgments or hypotheses about the person. We silently place each other on some rung of the invisible ladder called "status." We put each other in the proper income bracket. We visualize the home, the possessions, the circle of friends. We feel a twinge of either superiority or inferiority. We are not always proud of these reactions, but they are like automatic, conditioned reflexes.

Another way of putting it is that our work is closely tied to our self-esteem. From our earliest years we have learned that studying hard, working hard and being successful are the marks of a "good" person. The job is a symbol of all this. It tells ourselves and the world that we either have or don't have "the right stuff," that we have or have not fulfilled the expectations of our social group. Depending on our job position, we position our very self-identity somewhere along the success-failure continuum, and make corresponding value judgments about ourselves.

Very few people, it seems, ever stop to question this whole set of assumptions and social arrangements. They are content to conclude that "this is the way things are" and try to fit in as best they can. But there have always been philosophers and social critics who raise questions about the link between occupation and personhood. What happens, for example, to people whose limited intelligence or harsh environment precludes the possibility of moving up the educational and occupational ladder? Are they therefore failures as persons? Or less valuable? And what happens when a man is no longer able to work? There is no security against accident, illness, being laid off or forced into early retirement. Does a man lose dignity and self-worth at the same time that he loses his job? What is today called "midlife crisis" often begins when a man starts to feel threatened by the pack of younger, more aggressive men and women moving up to replace him.

Moreover, even those who survive the struggle for success do so at a high cost. Increased pressure to perform well, to increase sales and show profits at the shareholders' meetings creates an enormous amount of stress for many workers. So do longer hours, lack of cooperation, restrictions on freedom and creativity, infighting and jealousies between individuals and among departments, fear of shutdowns and mergers with accompanying layoffs or transfers, unclear lines of authority and accountability—these are the kinds of tensions I hear about from men who are working in what are often regarded as good or even prestigious jobs.

Some months ago the cover of *Esquire* magazine caught my eye. It seemed to sum up for me many of the myths about work that our society proclaims. The cover showed a man running at high speed, briefcase clutched in one hand. The caption read:

> SUCCESS!
> It is the religion of the '80s
> Everyone pursues it.
> Only the most driven and talented achieve it.
> Few know how to live without it—or with it.

Even granting that the message is deliberately exaggerated, think of what it is saying. Surely there is nothing wrong with success in itself. But when we make a religion out of it, we are asking of it something it cannot give—ultimate meaning, final answers to the great questions of human existence. Success then becomes an absolute, and all other values, including human persons, become relative and secondary.

The point is: Thoughtful people today are dissatisfied with some of the views of work propounded by our culture. They are saying, "Look, my work is important to me. But I don't want to be dominated by it, I don't want to let it make me sick, and I don't want to make it my god. Is there a better way? Do the scriptures or the church have anything meaningful to say about this important area of my life?"

A Christian Vision of Work

The answer is a ringing yes. In September of 1981, Pope John Paul II published a lengthy encyclical letter with the title *Laborem*

Exercens, "On Human Work." In it he reviewed some of the biblical insights and the church's theological reflections on the meaning of human labor. In the very first pages of the book of Genesis, the pope says, we find the source of the church's conviction that "work is a fundamental dimension of human existence on earth" (n. 4). It is not correct to think of work as an afterthought, as a punishment inflicted by God for sin. The view expressed in Genesis is much more positive. Even before sin enters the picture, man and woman are given the task of exercising "dominion" over the rest of God's creation (Gn 1:28-30). Today we would use the word "stewardship." The vocation to work is even more clear in Genesis 2:15, where it states that "the Lord God took the man and settled him in the garden of Eden to cultivate and care for it." In this primitive story of our human origins, the sacred writer is trying to express a profound truth: We humans have been given the responsibility to develop the resources of our earth in creative ways, and to do so with reverence and care.

There is another, even more profound way of putting this truth: God has chosen to make us partners with him in the ongoing mystery of creation. By studying the secrets of nature, by harnessing the powers and energies latent in the universe, human beings are privileged to cooperate with God's plan "to cultivate and care for the earth." Thereby they glorify God and contribute to the betterment of human life. In that sense, there is truly a sacred dimension to human work. I love to read Chapter 38 of the book of Sirach in this light. It starts out by praising the work of the physician and the pharmacist, saying that through their healing skills "God's creative work continues without cease" (vs. 8). Then it describes the work of engravers, designers, metal workers and potters, concluding with the beautiful thought that "they maintain God's ancient handiwork, and their concern is for the exercise of their skill" (vs. 34). What a positive vision of human labor: Work is not only a means of earning money; it is even more a way of developing our potential and of sharing in God's creative activity, participating in a mystery greater than ourselves.

Think of the implications of this. When human beings discover cures for disease, when they find healing therapies for mental and emotional distress, when they produce better and safer modes of transportation, when they improve agricultural methods, when they build cleaner and healthier cities, when they find better ways of communicating and processing information, when they equip all citizens with the knowledge and skills they need for meaningful employment—in these and thousands of other ways they are engaging in tasks that are truly sacred, because they are fulfilling the plan of God.

Another implication is this: If we as human beings are called to perfect the world in accord with the divine plan, then it is important that we regard our gifts and abilities as something entrusted to us by God. We are not to waste, squander, or misuse them. Rather, we are to develop and utilize them to the best of our ability. It is true that no one ever gets to use all of his or her potential. We are limited, and we have to make choices. I have always been bothered by the fact that I cannot do everything that I want to do. I have often been told, for example, that I have a gift for writing. I think I believe that myself, yet this is the first full-length book I have ever written. I have always enjoyed and been busy with other things like teaching, preaching and counseling. Some of our gifts will have to remain undeveloped, simply because we have established other priorities.

What saddens me, though, is when I see talented people choosing to live at a level far below their potential. They never read seriously, never take a class, never watch an educational program on television, never deepen their understanding of their religion. They remind me of the man in the gospel who, out of fear and resentment, went out and buried his master's money instead of working with it. "Play it safe, don't take chances" is a good way to avoid failure, but it is also a formula for staying only half alive.

Work and Human Dignity

So far we have been saying that human work has value because it is a participation in the creative activity of God and because it is a means of developing our unique personality. In his encyclical, Pope John Paul lifts up another aspect of work for our contemplation: Work takes its value not so much from what it produces, but from the dignity of the one doing it. The pope reminds us that Jesus Christ, the incarnate Son of God, "devoted most of the years of his life on earth to manual work at the carpenter's bench." The basis for determining the value of work, the pope says, "is not primarily the kind of work being done, but the fact that one who is doing it is a person" (n. 6). John Paul II never tires of proclaiming the dignity of the human person, created "in the image and likeness of God." Later in the encyclical, the pope uses this fundamental truth to denounce all attempts to dehumanize work, all ideologies that would make workers inferior to their products or to systems of domination and control, all attempts to divide people into classes of higher and lower status on the basis of their productivity.

What the pope is saying, it seems to me, is that work must always harmonize with human dignity. That means we are to work responsibly and ethically, in accord with God's own design for human beings. I think there are several implications here. For one thing, our work must not do harm to ourselves. This was one of the purposes of the Sabbath rest in the Old Testament. God asked his human creatures to quit working for one day a week in order to recall their own dignity as God's beloved people. Interestingly, modern medicine has identified what are called "Type A" personalities— highly driven, competitive people who can't seem to stop working and who are very vulnerable to stress-related diseases. I have given a number of workshops on "burnout" in the helping professions and have seen the emotional and spiritual wreckage that can overtake good people who drive themselves beyond their limits. I have also become angry when I listen to people who are forced by circumstances (company demands, low wages, etc.) to work in ways that are disruptive of any kind of balanced human life. Pope John Paul put it so well when he wrote, "However true it may be that man is destined for work and is called to it, in the first place work is always for man, and not man for work" (n. 6).

Secondly, to work humanly means that our work must not do harm to others. The Old Testament prophets were always challenging their fellow Israelites for their unjust practices: not paying their employees a decent wage, overworking them, defrauding their customers (e.g., Isaiah 58:3-4; Amos 8:4-6). Today one hears all too often the attitude, "I do my work and don't ask any questions." But is that really adequate for a Christian? Even if my work is good and harmless in itself, what if it is part of a larger system that has negative consequences for other people? I have talked with men who went to their employers with complaints about unethical practices; sometimes they were able to effect a change for the better, but other times they were demoted or fired. Just last night I talked on the phone to a man who was asked to fill out forms with false information about the company; when he refused, he was told he would either have to go on a different shift or take a cut in pay. He took the cut rather than be away from his family in the evening hours. I have read about people who quit their lucrative jobs when they realized they were directly involved in making nuclear weapons components. Others have protested or quit when they found that the company was doing nothing to stop its pollution of the environment. I have deep admiration for people like this. I am not saying that the action always has to be dramatic. I am saying that work often involves ethical issues and decisions that a conscientious Christian cannot lightly evade.

Work as Idolatry

Thirdly, and perhaps most important of all, to work humanly means that our work must not become an idol. That is, it must not become so all-absorbing that it displaces all other realities, including God, from the very center of our lives. It has often been noted that the first commandment of the Decalogue is the most important of all: "I am the Lord your God; you shall not have other gods besides me." The Old Testament prophets would often warn the people not to fall down in worship before the works of their own hands: "Every artisan is put to shame by his idol: He has molded a fraud, without breath of life. Nothing are they, a ridiculous work . . ." (Jer 10:14-15). The prophets, of course, were talking about the ancient Hebrews' tendency to exchange the worship of God for the idol worship of the pagan nations around them. But that image comes to my mind every time I see TV commercials showing people practically bowing down in adoration before the latest model car or computer, or whatever.

More seriously, I have seen too many good men who make a god out of their work. Sometimes they are driven by financial pressures. They think the only way they and their family can be comfortable is by putting in the extra hours and extra efforts. Other times they feel the pressure from their superiors in the company. It would not be their choice to work so much, they say, but what can you do when the boss keeps reminding you that there are plenty of others around who would be glad to replace you! I have a great deal of compassion for these men, and I don't have any easy answers for their situation. But I always ask them to look at it in light of their Christian beliefs. I ask them to pay attention to what is happening to their life as a whole: to their health, their marriage and family life, their needs for relaxation, their spiritual life. Sometimes, after going through that process, a man will end up telling me, "Look, this is no way to live. I'm paying too high a price. I think my family and I can learn to live with less." Or, "I'm going to talk to my boss about lightening my load. If we can't work something out, I'll trust God to help me find another job." Somehow, in their prayer and honest reflection, these men come to understand something of what Jesus was saying: Don't work so hard "for food that perishes, but for the food that endures for eternal life" (Jn 6:27).

I have also seen men for whom work has become idolatrous, not because of external pressure, but because they have become addicted to it. The excitement, the challenge, the adventure, the sense of achievement, the recognition—all can become high and heady, an intoxicating trip that runs on its own energy source. This can happen in the business world, the helping professions, the creative arts, sales and marketing, research and other positions. What happens is that the man overworks by his own choice because the satisfactions are so intrinsic and immediate. In my experience, it is very difficult for him even to recognize what is happening. He will laugh it off if you suggest that he is becoming a workaholic. Unfortunately, it usually takes some kind of negative experience to wake him up: a major failure (the idol collapses), a breakdown of health, an alienated wife, a child who gets into trouble. At that moment, we can only hope that some compassionate person will be there to help him pick up the pieces and rebuild his life, this time with God at the center. "But seek first the kingdom [of God] and his righteousness," Jesus said, "and all these things will be given you besides" (Mt 6:33).

Let's pause a moment now and survey the territory we've covered. We've been saying that work is part of God's plan for his human creatures. Work unites us to God's creative plan for the unfolding of the universe; at the same time, it contributes to the fulfillment of our own personality. Work carries with it certain ethical responsibilities: It should better ourselves and others, not do us harm; it should reverence the environment, not destroy it. And work is not to become a substitute for God or for healthy human relationships.

Christian Attitudes at Work

Following from these basic insights, as I have gleaned them from Pope John Paul's encyclical, I believe there are several other attitudes that Christians are called to manifest in their work. One of them is the striving for excellence. By that I do not mean "winning at all costs" or "beating the competition." I'm talking about giving one's best effort to the job, as opposed to the shoddy, careless workmanship that so many people complain about today.

A few months ago I had to take my car into the garage to have some work done on the engine. The mechanic was a true craftsman who enjoyed his work and took pride in it. He was a walking encyclopedia of knowledge about car engines and he took care to explain to me everything he was doing and why. Most of the time I was lost, but it was a real pleasure to be served by a man like that. While he was working, a teenage boy came in and said to him, "When could you work on my engine? My Dad says you're the best in the business." That little incident made me realize something else: When a worker does strive for excellence, the word gets around. Here is a person you can trust, one who will respect you and not try to manipulate you. I believe that kind of attitude comes from a reverence for God and for the dignity of human persons.

Another attitude Christians are called to manifest in their work is a genuine caring for people. The best managers and supervisors have learned (sometimes the hard way) that it is far better to encourage people's strengths than to pound on their weaknesses. Successful salespeople will prefer to lose the sale rather than the customer's good will. To me it is not surprising that the Golden Rule of the gospel has been taken over into the stated philosophy of many businesses and corporations: "Treat others the way you would want them to treat you" (Mt 7:12). Jesus understood human nature; so his teachings and commandments, while they may demand a lot of us, are ultimately for our own growth and betterment.

But what are Christians to do when they work in an environment that does not embody these attitudes? What if there is suspicion and mistrust running through the organization? What about dishonesty, cheating, violations of ethics? What about profane and obscene language? What about jealousies, infighting, back-stabbing? What if company practices are not in line with their own statement of philosophy?

Again, there are no simple answers to these questions. At a minimum, a Christian has an obligation not to become part of the problem. We are called to resist these evils, at least by not participating in them. Sometimes there is more we can do. For instance, we can talk

with other workers to see whether, in their honest moments, they too
are troubled by what they see. In this way they might work out strategies for using their collective influence to bring about some changes.
I'm afraid we Christians are often too self-protective, too fearful of
"rocking the boat," so that we permit unjust and hurtful situations to
go on and on. Sometimes it only takes a little initiative on our part to
bring about some constructive change in the workplace.

But what if we have to act alone, because nobody will join us?
Even here, I believe, we have to rely on the strength that God alone
can provide. Our church history is filled with examples of saints and
others who stood up for what was right, even though the risk was
great. I'm not saying there is an obligation to do this in every instance. A man may, after prayer and thoughtful reflection, come to
the honest conclusion that he is truly powerless to effect a change,
and that the only outcome of his action would be to bring further
harm on himself and his family. What I am saying is that we need to
honestly struggle with these issues, not just walk away from them or
claim they are none of our business. I am always challenged when I
read what Peter wrote to the early Christians: "Who now is going to
harm you if you are enthusiastic for what is good? But even if you
should suffer because of righteousness, blessed are you. For it is better to suffer for doing good, if that be the will of God, than for doing
evil" (1 Pt 3:13-14,17).

The Place of Leisure

I would like to end this chapter by saying a few things about the
other side of work: leisure. According to the Bible, human beings are
not to be dominated either by work or by leisure. Rather, they are to
image God the Creator, who worked for six days and then rested on
the seventh. So God gave the Hebrew people a very gentle, sane commandment: "Remember to keep holy the sabbath day. Six days you
may labor and do all your work, but the seventh day is the sabbath of
the LORD, your God. No work may be done then either by you, or by
your son or daughter . . ." (Ex 20:8-10). The purpose of the sabbath
rest, then, was twofold: to give men and women a break from their
work and to remind them of their dignity as God's beloved people.
Christians of the New Testament reinterpreted the commandment in
light of the central mystery of their faith: the resurrection of Jesus

Christ. So now Sunday, the first day of the week, became for them the day to rest from their labors and to gather for communal worship of God in the liturgy of the Mass.

Without this rhythm of work and rest, labor and leisure, our lives would become impoverished. We would easily forget the purpose of our existence. We would lose our spiritual center. We would neglect our most important relationships: God and each other. So a spirituality of work must also include a spirituality of leisure.

It is all too easy for men in today's society to ignore this necessary balance between work and leisure. Some men (and from conversations I have had, their number seems to be increasing) have never developed a healthy work ethic. They are fixated at the stage of boyhood, where life is a series of games and recreations to be enjoyed, interrupted occasionally by the annoying necessity of work. There is no real commitment to work, no pride in a job well done. Employers complain about men who try to get away with doing as little as possible. Wives complain about husbands who refuse to involve themselves in the ordinary tasks of keeping up a home or raising a family. Boys who used to spend hours and hours watching television have become adult men who spend hours and hours watching television. Boys who spent their time hanging around the arcades and shopping malls have become men who hang around bars with "the boys." Others, obsessed with the thought that they might be missing something at life's smorgasbord, spend all their leisure cramming in a series of trips, outings and diversions. I have seen some of these men come to midlife with a deep sense of guilt for having wasted their life. They are the luckier ones, because there is still time for change. Even more pathetic are those who never stop pursuing the shallow, self-indulgent life.

But if there are a sizable number of men for whom leisure is the supreme good, there are perhaps even more who worship at the altar of work. Their unbalanced lives leave no room for needed recreation or even physical rest. They drive themselves, or allow themselves to be driven, by the demands of their jobs. I am not talking about men who simply have to work more than a 40-hour week because of financial circumstances or temporary work requirements. I'm talking about men who work far more than they would really have to and who are thereby not respecting the rhythm between work and leisure intended by the Creator. Often the price they are paying is evident to everyone but themselves: physical and mental fatigue, high blood pressure, digestive problems, sleep disturbance, irritability, depression, strained relationships with wife and children, loss of a sense of humor.

Avoiding Burnout

I have a great deal of compassion for these men: first, because they are generally very good men; and secondly, because I have been there myself. It is often said that the phenomenon of burnout is especially rampant in the helping professions. I believe that I came within inches of burnout myself some years ago. I purposely kept some pages from my appointment book from that time as a reminder of what I had been doing to myself. Now I look at it and wonder how—and why—I ever kept up such a pace. But it caught up with me. I began to notice some things that were happening to me. I've always been a healthy person, but I found myself getting frequent colds, almost like one after another. I'm a generally easygoing man, yet I was getting more and more irritable. Everything was getting to me, and I found myself slipping into a dull apathy. Still I pressed on doggedly. What finally got my attention was a terrific chest pain that kept me up all night. I went to the doctor the next morning. He told me it was only a muscle spasm in the middle of my back; but he went on to say, "You're wound up tight as a spring; you'd better learn to relax." The incident was enough to scare me into some soul-searching. I came to see that in pushing myself so hard I was actually being disobedient to my own body and emotions; I was stretching them beyond their limits to satisfy my own illusion of boundless energy. I had to accept my limits, set some priorities and let some things go. It was hard, but I have never regretted it. And it wasn't long before my good health and mental peace returned.

There are many possible motivations for overwork. Some men simply enjoy their job and work more at it than they have to because it has its own reward. But there may be other, less noble, motivations. Some men have really been caught up in the materialism trap. They work the equivalent of two jobs because they see it is as the only way to finance the kind of home, car, lake property, travel and other perks that they have come to see as essential for their well-being. Unfortunately, they have never learned the simple joys of walking through a nature park, reading a good book, or an evening of stimulating conversation with friends.

Other men drive themselves at work in a never-ending attempt to reassure themselves of their inner worth. They keep trying to achieve some standard of success that is forever eluding them. Often they are men who never experienced themselves as lovable and valuable simply for who they are. Somehow they felt they never measured up to what their parents expected of them, and now their work compulsion is a desperate attempt to prove themselves—if not to the parent, at least to themselves. For even if the parents are absent or deceased, the perfectionism has been internalized and exercises its own tyranny from within. "If only I can achieve this goal, then I will be at peace." But always a new goal emerges, and the process continues relentlessly.

Other men may use work as a means of avoiding some other issues in their lives. Often these are men who are talented, responsible workers and even managers. But they feel inadequate when it comes to relationships, particularly intimate ones. When such men marry and have children, they are not ready to deal with the emotional demands that such relationships entail. So the easiest course to follow is avoidance, and the world of work provides a perfect cover for them.

Much of this functions at the unconscious level, of course, so that the real agendas are seldom perceived well enough to be dealt with. What appears is something like the following (and I wonder how many thousands of times this kind of scene occurs in living rooms and kitchens around the country each day):

Wife: "Dear, there's something we really need to talk about."

Husband: "Can't we settle it right here?"

Wife: "No—it's too important; we're going to need some time."

Husband: "Look, you know this is a busy time for me—they're counting on me to get these reports in at work. Why don't you handle it yourself?"

Wife: "There you go again! Always it's your work! When are you ever going to become part of this family?" (She bursts into tears and goes to the bedroom).

And the man walks out the door muttering that he will never understand women.

We need to look at this issue a little more closely. What we have here is not a selfish man or an uncaring man. He really does love his wife and children. What we have here is a fearful man. He is afraid of conflict, afraid of strong emotions. The schools he attended have taught him well how to think clearly and plan carefully. They have taught him how to make a good impression and how to assess other people. But for the most part, no one has taught him about the care and feeding of close relationships—the skills of intimacy. No one has taught him how to deal with strong emotions—his own and others. We will be saying more about this in the next chapter. For now, I am simply saying that society makes it easy for men to avoid problems and issues they are reluctant to face.

Whatever the reasons for overinvestment in work—excitement, financial success, building self-esteem, avoiding relationship problems—the result is the same: an unbalanced life. We are developing one part of our personality at the expense of some others. And that is a distortion of our nature. It is disobedience to the plan of God. It is a failure to live spiritually. I am not saying this to send us off on another guilt trip. I am calling for an honest look at ourselves. If instead of a gentle rhythm between work and leisure, we are careening out of control in one direction or the other, it is never too late to bring ourselves back into balance. It is another form of "conversion" that we talked about in the last chapter.

St. Thomas Aquinas had some refreshing things to say about all this. He once wrote that no one can live without some pleasure; that is why, if one is deprived of all innocent pleasures, he will inevitable drift into sinful ones. How wise. "All work and no play" can set us up for a good binge of self-pity and, eventually, self-indulgence. I have seen that insidious pattern in myself. So, while I still put in a full day's work, I try to make sure I always have something enjoyable or relaxing to look forward to: some classical music, a walk outside, reading the paper and having a beer at the end of the day. The same with the week: I can keep busy and be creative if I can look forward to a couple of favorite TV shows and a bridge game with friends at the end of the week.

It sounds simple, but it works for me.

5

The Quest for Love

We have been saying all along that spirituality is not something added on to life; rather, it is something that permeates life. It is a fundamental attitude or vision about life, one that becomes the basis for making everyday decisions. We have defined spirituality as "the ongoing endeavor to respond to our relationship with God." In the last two chapters, we tried to connect spirituality with two basic dimensions of our life: self-esteem and work. In the present chapter we want to link up with another key dimension of life—our search for love.

Originally I was going to title this chapter "Marriage and Family." But then I realized that a number of my readers would be either not married or not parents. Some will be single, some divorced, some widowed. And I think I can presume that some will be homosexual, and for them marriage will not be in their future plans. I would like it to be known that while I believe that homosexual acts are morally wrong, I believe just as firmly that homosexuals have both the need and the capacity for human love, as well as for genuine spirituality. So I am hoping that what follows in this chapter will be applicable to anyone who is struggling with questions of love and intimacy from a Christian viewpoint.

Let's start with our basic human experience. It is no secret that the need for love is probably the strongest drive within our personality. Back in the 1930s the brilliant psychoanalyst Karen Horney hypothesized that every newborn infant experiences what she called "basic anxiety." She described it as "the feeling of being alone and helpless in a potentially hostile world." To counteract basic anxiety, the infant needs the warm, caring presence of other human persons. Children who grow up without stable, loving people around them will be vulnerable to anxiety all their lives, Horney believed. Furthermore, all human beings have this built-in desire for relationship, for connectedness with another or others. In any case, our experiences of loneliness are powerful testimonies to "the quest for love."

The Bible and Love

We have been saying all along that spirituality includes a vision of reality as well as a lifestyle based on that vision. The vision needs to be grounded ultimately in the great truths of our Christian faith. So what does our faith have to say about the quest for love? First of all, that it is God-given. Our need for love is not merely the product of biological evolution. The Bible pictures God gazing upon his first human creature and saying, "It is not good for the man to be alone" (Gn 2:18). How true. Our separateness, our uniqueness, is only one side of us; the other side is our longing for relationship and for communion. Indeed, this is one of the great challenges of life: How do we achieve communion without losing our individuality? In any case, we have a deep need to know that we are loved.

Which brings us to another great truth of our faith: God himself answers this need of ours by offering us his own love. In the New Testament, the First Letter of John is a long, lingering contemplation of this incredible mystery:

> See what love the Father has
>   bestowed on us . . . (3:1).
> In this way the love of God was
>   revealed to us:
> God sent his only Son into the world so
> that we might have life through him (4:9).
> In this is love: not that
> we have loved God, but that
> he loved us and sent his Son as expiation
>   for our sins (4:10).
> We have come to know and to believe
>   in the love God has for us (4:16).

I referred to this truth as a mystery because there is simply no adequate explanation for why God should love us. He certainly is not lonely, since he is the very fullness of life and being shared by three divine persons. Clearly he does not need us for his own completion, since he contains all perfection within himself. All we can say is that, freely and graciously, God wants to share his goodness, his happi-

ness, his very life with us, his human creatures: "With age-old love I
have loved you" (Jer 31:3). We can almost hear God saying, as Wal-
ter Cronkite used to say on the evening news, "And that's the way it
is!" When confronted with this reality of God's love, it is not ours to
try and figure it out. We have only two choices: to accept it or reject
it. We will come back to this later.

There is another awesome side to this mystery of God's love: It is
unconditional. This means that it is not dependent on our earning it or
paying for it; it is an utterly free gift. We might be able to manipulate
our friends or even our families into loving us, but we cannot do that
with God. His love is simply there, available to us for the receiving.
"Unconditional" also means that God will not withdraw his love when
we don't respond, or when we respond unlovingly. This is a hard notion for us to grasp, since our own love is so often dependent on how
the other person responds to us. Maybe that is why the scriptures are so
persistent on this point: God's commitment to us is firm and absolute:

> "I will never forsake you, or abandon you" (Heb 13:5).
> Though the mountains leave their place
> and the hills be shaken,
> My love shall never leave you,
> nor my covenant of peace be shaken,
>   says the LORD . . . (Is 54:10).

> For I am convinced that neither death nor life . . . nor any other
> creature will be able to separate us from the love of God in
> Christ Jesus our Lord (Rom 8:38-39).

But surely our sins will separate us from God's love? No, the Bible says. Even our sins don't have that kind of power, as long as we
are willing to repent of them. In the parable of the Prodigal Son, Jesus pictures God as the loving father who waits for his wayward son
to return home, runs to meet him and puts on a feast to celebrate his
homecoming. And John the disciple writes so beautifully:

> If we say: "We are without sin," we deceive
> ourselves and the truth is not in us.
> If we acknowledge our sins, he
> is faithful and just and will forgive
> our sins and cleanse us
> from every wrongdoing (1 Jn 1: 8-9).

Really, then, the only thing that can thwart God's love for us is our refusal to accept it.

But why would anyone refuse this kind of gracious, unconditional love? The answer is simple: We suspect it will cost us something. And we are right. To accept God's love into our hearts calls for a response on our part. It calls us to love in return. St. John tells us,

> Beloved, if God so loved us,
> we also must love one another (1 Jn 4:11).

In other words, we are not just to receive God's love passively; we are to spread it around to our brothers and sisters. In that sense, God really does need us, because we are the only human, visible signs of his love and presence in the world today. Think about it: How did you come to know God's love? Probably prayer and scripture reading helped, but most likely your deepest experience of God's love came through the love of certain other people in your life. They mediated God's love to you in a human way, in a way you were able to receive it. You came to believe that you were lovable, and that opened you up to the ultimate source of all love: God. That's why John the disciple says so clearly,

> No one has ever seen God.
> Yet if we love one another
> God remains in us,
> and his love is brought to perfection in us (1 Jn. 4:12).

That is, our love for others can actually become an "epiphany," a revelation of God to them.

God's love for us, then, is both a gift and a call, both an answer to our need for love and a challenge to share love with others. Sometimes, when I hear people speak of the unconditional love of God, I get the impression of a God who is an indifferent wimp. That is, he keeps being nice to us even if we ignore him. But that's not the God of the scriptures. The Bible shows us a God who deeply, passionately cares about whether and how we respond to his love. He asks us to make choices. Persistent refusal to love can only lead to the deadening of our personality, and eventually to eternal death. Whereas wholehearted commitment to love God and our neighbor is the only way to fullness of life.

What Does It Mean to Love?

At some point, of course, the question has to arise: What does it mean to love others? Here we could get into a hairy discussion of the kinds and degrees of love, the opinions of various philosophers, and so forth. But for our purposes, I would like to lift up for our meditation a provocative statement that Jesus made at the Last Supper:

> "This is my commandment:
> love one another
> as I love you" (Jn 15:12).

So, the best way to learn the meaning of love in the Christian sense would be to study the gospels and see how Jesus loved the people he encountered.

But let's take another direction for the moment. One of the best definitions of love that I have ever seen is given by psychiatrist M. Scott Peck in his book *The Road Less Traveled*. "Love," he says, "is the will to extend one's self for the purpose of nurturing one's own or another's spiritual growth." Let's take a closer look at that. First of all, we should not take the word "spiritual" in a strictly religious sense. Peck is talking about anything that helps to make a person more fully human. "Spiritual growth," then, would include things like increased self-esteem, sense of worth, freedom from ignorance and fear, ability to form friendships, sense of responsibility. Any time we help ourselves or others to grow in these directions, we are loving.

Note the emphasis on "will" rather than "feeling." Here is where so many people get tripped up: They mistake the feeling of love for the activity of love. Scott Peck uses the example of the tearful alcoholic telling the bartender how much he loves his family—yet he neither supports them nor spends time with them. Feelings, intentions, desires are not enough; love requires decision and action. Note also that the definition speaks of "extending one's self." The very nature of love is to move beyond the boundaries of one's own ego, to become actively concerned about the growth and well-being of someone else. That's what people mean when they say that "love is giving." Finally, Scott Peck includes "nurturing one's own" spiritual growth as well as someone else's. That is, the definition includes healthy love of self as well as love of others. But he is also saying that there is a mutuality about true love: Extending myself in order to nurture another's spiritual growth also enriches me; if it does not, there is probably something defective about my love.

I would like to expand a bit on this. Recently a book came out by Robin Norwood with the interesting title *Women Who Love Too Much*. Personally I would have given it a different title, because strictly speaking it's impossible to love too much. But she is writing about a very real phenomenon: women who keep giving of themselves to men who abuse their love, ignore them, mistreat them, manipulate them and break every promise they make. Yet these women allow such behavior to go on and on. Externally it may look like heroic love, but in reality it is not; it is not nurturing anyone's spiritual growth. The woman is suffering intensely, and the man is not being helped to examine or change his unloving behavior. To give in to another's unreasonable demands is not an act of love but of masochism.

But neither is it true love when I extend myself for you and then demand that you reciprocate: "I'll scratch your back if you scratch mine." We have all seen that kind of love in action, especially when it takes the form of inducing guilt in the other: "How could you refuse that for me after all I've done for you!" Ordinarily, of course, we can expect that our acts of love will elicit a positive response in the other, at least in the form of gratitude. But what if a response is not forthcoming? Do I then go into a tirade, or a pout, or a binge of self-pity, or a smoldering resentment that finds expression in little digs and cuts of sarcasm? There is a tough test of my love.

The truth is, some people who need our love are temporarily or maybe even permanently incapable of returning it. It is then that we are called to image the unconditional love of God. For instance, children and adolescents may be so developmentally self-centered that they simply take our love for granted. The elderly may find fault with everything we try to do for them. The emotionally hurt may be so wary that they have to continually test our love. The poor may be so beaten down that they are unable to respond. If you have ever watched a film of Mother Teresa, you will know what I mean. In her work among "the poorest of the poor" she seldom experiences any evidence of reward or success; yet her face and those of her sisters are radiant with serenity and simple joy. Their own spiritual good is being nurtured, Scott Peck would say, because they believe they are being faithful to what God is calling them to do.

Of course, sometimes "love has to be tough," as Christian psychologist Dr. James Dobson would say. That is, we may have to seriously challenge someone who is falling into a pattern of laziness or irresponsibility: "Look, you have so much potential, but I don't see you using any of it. You're just sitting around and letting life pass you by. Can we talk?" Or, we may have to set limits on someone who is stepping out of line. Yet, when done with care and respect, these are genuine acts of love: "the will to extend ourselves for the sake of nurturing our own or another's spiritual good." But that takes effort, and it's often much easier to be Mr. Nice Guy and let things ride. But that's negligence, not love.

As a matter of fact, I have often thought of love as a blend of affirmation-plus-challenge. One without the other is inadequate. If I keep telling you how wonderful you are but never tell you how your faults annoy me, my love will be dishonest and sentimental. If I keep challenging you to face up to your problems but never affirm your good qualities, you will soon become discouraged. If I really love you, I will want to tell you about the good I see in you, about your strengths and your potential. I will want you to believe in yourself, to know that I believe in you and will stand by you. But I will also want you to know your limitations and your blind spots. I will want you to take responsibility for your own life and growth and to use your God-given abilities in accordance with his plan. And I know that this is how I would like to be treated by those who say they love me.

I said before that if we really want to understand the meaning of love, we need to study the gospels and see how Jesus embodied love in action, how he extended himself in order to nurture the spiritual good of others. We would see, for example, how he treated each person as an individual and with dignity and respect: Nicodemus the Pharisee (Jn 3:1-21), the pagan centurion (Mt 8:5-13), the chronic invalid (Jn 5:1-15). We would see how he accepted even sinners and gently invited them to conversion: the paralyzed man (Mt 9:1-8), Levi and his friends (Mk 2:14-17), the Samaritan woman (Jn 4:4-30). We would see how he affirmed and encouraged his disciples (Lk 10:17-24), and how he also challenged them to let go of their petty ambitions (Mk 12:38-45). And we would see how he continued to reach out to those who opposed him and how he extended forgiveness to them with his last breath (Lk 23:32-34). Indeed, the generous, self-giving love of Jesus Christ is the source of life-long meditation for Christians who are trying to grow in love. It is the pattern, the model, on which they base their own efforts to love. Or more accurately, they are deeply aware that their own efforts to love as Jesus did will always be inadequate; instead, they ask him to manifest his own love through them.

Love in Marriage

The above remarks about love can be applied, I believe, to all of our relationships, including our families, our work associates and our friends. But now I would like to share some reflections on love in the specific context of marriage. Being a committed celibate, I realize I will be speaking from limited perspective. At the same time, I have spent a lot of time listening to married couples, both as friends and as counselees. I have often been asked to help people who are trying to rebuild their lives after a broken marriage. I am now at a point where I would like to share some of my reflections.

Let's start with the word of God. From the very beginning, the scriptures make it clear that marriage is not merely a human invention; it comes from the heart of God himself. In the book of Genesis, marriage is seen as a remedy for human loneliness. God gazes upon the human creature he has fashioned and says, "It is not good for the man to be alone. I will make a suitable partner for him" (Gn 2:18). And God proceeds to create woman, brings her to the man, and blesses their intimate union of body and spirit: "That is why a man leaves his father and mother and clings to his wife, and the two of them become one body" (Gn 2:24).

There are many passages in the Old Testament that speak of the goodness of human love and marriage. When Jacob fell in love with Laban's daughter Rachel, Laban promised her to Jacob if he would go to work for him. "So Jacob served seven years for Rachel," the Bible says, "yet they seemed to him but a few days because of his love for her" (Gn 29:20). And there is that famous passage in the book of Sirach:

> Happy the husband of a good wife,
> twice-lengthened are his days.
> A worthy wife brings joy to her husband,
> peaceful and full is his life.
> A good wife is a generous gift
> bestowed upon him who fears the LORD;
> Be he rich or poor, his heart is content,
> and a smile is ever on his face (Sir 26:1-4).

Like much of the Bible, the viewpoint is from the male side; but there is no doubt that the scriptures see marriage as intended by God to bring wholeness and fulfillment to both partners (see, for example, the book of Ruth or Tobit).

Later, the prophets began to use the image of marriage to describe the relationship, the covenant, between God and his chosen people. God is seen as a husband who cannot stay angry at his wife even when she offends him:

> The LORD calls you back,
>> like a wife forsaken and grieved in spirit . . .
> For a brief moment I abandoned you,
>> but with great tenderness I will take you back.
> In an outburst of wrath, for a moment
>> I hid my face from you;
> But with enduring love I take pity on you,
>> says the LORD your redeemer (Is 54:6-8).

When Jesus came, even though he remained celibate, he continued to hold up marriage as a special sign of God's love and blessing in human life. He worked his first miracle at a wedding banquet, at the request of his mother, in order to spare the newlyweds and their families from embarrassment. He insisted that men and women not regard each other as mere sex objects (Mt 5:28), and he challenged the Pharisees to uphold God's original plan for marriage as a life-long commitment (Mt 19:3-9). After the resurrection of Christ, the Christians began to reflect on their relationship with Jesus and to realize that their spiritual union with him was in many ways similar to the intimate union of husband and wife. Or, perhaps more accurately, it was the other way around: The marriage bond was seen as a sign of the faithful, enduring, forgiving love of Christ for the church, his spouse. St. Paul recalls the passage from Genesis about the marital union between husband and wife and calls it "a great mystery, but I speak in reference to Christ and the church. In any case, each one of you should love his wife as himself, and the wife should respect her husband" (Eph 5:32-33).

A Spirituality of Marriage

All this rich biblical background forms the basis for a solid spirituality of marriage. We have to be a bit careful here. It is all too easy to spiritualize marriage, to imagine that the only time spirituality

comes into the picture in marriage is when family members pray or
read the Bible together. Let's remember what we said before: Spirituality is holistic. It embraces all of our life and activity. Spirituality
in marriage means that everything the couple does—from their
budget-planning to their sexual lovemaking—has the potential to
deepen their relationship with God. That is the beautiful, liberating
truth that Christian couples are called to live out.

Before the Second Vatican Council, many thoughtful Catholics
were feeling that the church had somewhat lost touch with the biblical roots of its teaching on marriage. Not only that, but it had lost
touch with the day-to-day lives of married Christians. So the
church's teaching often came off sounding otherworldly and remote
from real life; or it seemed legalistic and preoccupied with what was
sinful and what was O.K., especially in matters of sex.

So, before the council convened, the bishops and theologians
made it a point to consult with married lay people and to listen to
their experiences and their concerns. That's why there is such a positive and inspiring chapter on marriage and the family in the council's
Pastoral Constitution on the Church in the Modern World (nn. 41-
42). The former Code of Canon Law used to define marriage as a
contract whereby the partners give to each other exclusive rights over
each other's bodies for those acts that lead to the procreation of children. This was a roundabout way of saying, "Marriage is about sexual intercourse—period."

But the council's vision of marriage is much more holistic. Marriage, the council says, is "an intimate communion of life and love."
Think of the implications of that. First of all, it certainly includes
sexual intercourse, but it's much more than that. It embraces all of
"life and love." That includes employment, homemaking, budget-
ing, child care, recreation, in-laws, and bad moods. Second, the
council calls marriage "an intimate communion," or "partnership."
The accent is on the sharing of life, wherein "the two shall be as one."
That is what every starry-eyed couple I've ever known dreams about
and talks about while they are dating. But unfortunately, some of
them move into marriage without realizing that "communion" requires some letting go of personal independence. The result is disas-
trous conflict. The council takes this communion very seriously and
sees it as the heart of marriage.

Let's take a closer look at this notion of intimate communion and its possible connection with spirituality. Author Dolores Curran has done a most valuable piece of research which she published in a book called *Traits of A Healthy Family*. She sent surveys to 500 professionals working with families. The survey consisted of 56 traits or behaviors that are typically found in healthy couples and families; she asked the professionals to check the 15 traits that they found most often or regarded as most typical of healthy families. Interestingly, many of the professionals were so intrigued by the study that they made copies of it and asked their colleagues to fill it out, too; as a result, Curran received more replies than she had sent out—551—something which never ever happens in a research study! But the main point is this: Out of those 56 traits, the professionals ranked "good communication" as the number one ingredient of a healthy family—even over such obvious favorites as sense of trust, sharing time, and respecting privacy. It is clear that people today regard good communication as the essential building-block of good relationships.

This fact is even more remarkable when we realize that it was not always so. As Dolores Curran says:

> It's intriguing to ponder the fact that this trait wasn't even considered an important marital trait a generation ago. Why? Why was communication and listening perceived by today's family professionals to be the single most important characteristic of health in the family today? One family counselor I surveyed answered the question for me when he said, "Because without communication you don't know one another. If you don't know one another, you don't care about one another—and that's what the family ballgame is all about."

And, I would add, that's what the marriage game is all about: knowing one another and caring about one another. In previous generations, as Curran suggests, couples didn't put that high a premium on communication. I suspect it was because they generally worked alongside each other, on the farm or in the family store, and communication came about rather naturally. They got to know each other and to experience mutual care just by struggling together to manage the farm or business, to provide food and shelter, to care for the children and to deal with sickness. But nowadays, with husband and wife working different jobs and with survival needs pretty well taken care of, those natural communication opportunities aren't

there. So couples have to "work at" communicating if they are going
to grow in their sense of knowing and caring about each other. This
presents new challenges, I think, particularly for males.

Difficulties in Communication

Both my reading and my experience of listening to married
couples have convinced me that contemporary American males are
not very successful at forming and sustaining close relationships.
They surely have no difficulty in attracting women or in sexual performance (although psychiatrists and others have noted an increase
in cases of functional impotence in men today). But what appears to
be lacking in many men is the capacity (or perhaps the willingness) to
share their personal thoughts, feelings and beliefs with their partner,
to listen and talk at a deeper level, to be comfortable with showing
emotion and with accepting emotion in the other. In short, their
communication skills are not well developed. Here is only a sample of
comments I have heard from women over the years:

"He doesn't let me know what he's thinking or feeling."

"We can have great intellectual discussions, but he won't talk
about anything personal."

"We talk a lot, but it's all very safe and superficial."

"I just can't seem to make him understand how I feel."

"He just can't deal with feelings—mine, the children's, his
own."

Note that these are not the comments of whining, disgruntled
wives who simply have unrealistic expectations of men. I have heard
them from mature, thoughtful women who deeply care about their
husbands and treasure the other good qualities they see in them. But
they are seeing a wound, a defect which would not have to be and
which blocks further growth in their relationship.

In an earlier chapter I hinted that the root of the problem is not
in the male's selfishness or bad will, but rather in his cultural conditioning. After all, what do we males learn, almost from day one?
That being masculine means being tough. And what does "tough"
mean? Well, it certainly means being physically strong, able to run
hard, play hard, take the hard knocks, endure the heat and the cold
and the rough terrain. Later on it comes to include being "tough-
minded"—that is, logical, rational, objective, clear-headed. It also

means being in control of our emotions. After all, the job has to get done, and we don't want any crybabies around who will feel hurt if things don't go their way.

All of which may serve us well in the competitive world of school, business, sports, or organization. But when it comes to close relationships, such as marriage, we're not well prepared. Why? Because an intimate relationship like marriage calls for a high degree of self-disclosure. Well, we're pretty good at swapping stories or having a good argument about sports or politics. But she wants to know how I really feel about her parents. What do I worry about? What do I think her girlfriend should do about that creep she's dating? How do I know? I never think about such things.

Which isn't quite true. We do think about them. But we don't talk about them. Nobody ever suggested we could or should. So we just push them to the back of our minds and get on with it. Now, all of a sudden (so it seems) the wife thinks it's awfully important that we start talking about some of these "deeper" things. What to do?

I'm not suggesting that this is the universal scenario. But it does illustrate what can easily become a series of "communication barriers" in a marriage. The point is: Many men have become distant from their own inner world of personal beliefs, values and feelings. We may not even realize that we are feeling anxious, or discouraged, or resentful, or threatened. Or that our voice is rising and our face is getting flushed. If we had been taught to pay attention to these inner signals, we would have some valuable data on which we could act. Or, if we are aware of them, we are not accustomed to talking about them. Instead, we bottle them up inside. I once read a book by psychologist Sidney Jourard called *The Transparent Self*, where he shows the value of self-awareness and self-disclosure. One very interesting chapter was entitled "Some Lethal Aspects of the Male Role." The author believes that the higher incidence of heart diseases, digestive disorders and circulatory problems in males is related to their inability or unwillingness to reveal their inner selves. They "hold everything inside" and it eats away at their vital organs.

Self-Disclosure

So here is the first building-block of good communication: being willing to share your inner thoughts and feelings with your wife. For instance, when a man comes home from work and his wife asks him,

"How was your day?" she will often hear, "Fine. What's for dinner?" End of conversation. But suppose you were to take that very natural occasion to say, "Well, a couple of good things happened—we did get that Johnson contract. But actually, I felt pretty tense all day. A couple of rumors are going around that there's going to be a major shakeup in our department. I don't know what it might mean for me." What you have just done is let your wife into a significant area of your life; you've taken a step toward "communion."

Now there are seemingly good reasons why men may not want to engage in this kind of self-disclosure. For one thing, they don't want to burden the wife with more problems. What I have found, though, is that problems can't be hidden from her anyway. Most women are intuitive enough to pick up the fact that something is troubling their man. And since the human mind (like most of nature) abhors a vacuum, she will try to find out what is bothering him. If he answers "Nothing," but his mood remains negative, she is likely to conclude that it must be something she has said or done. Behold the beginning of a communication breakdown and a barrier to intimacy.

Another problem with self-disclosure is that it can be risky. Your wife can take what you say and turn it against you. She can use it to criticize you, or ridicule you. After a few experiences like that, you want to keep things to yourself. But is that the only alternative? I don't think so. Here is where another communication skill is called for: honest challenge. What if you were to say to your wife, "Look, I just shared something that was important to me, and you don't take it seriously" (or, "You criticize me instead of trying to understand"). "That hurts, and it makes me want to clam up instead of communicate with you." Well, she might say, "There you go getting defensive again," and walk away. But there's just as good a chance that she will say, "I guess you're right. I didn't even realize I was doing that. I'm sorry—let's keep talking." Now you are bonding, growing in communion. And even if she does walk away, there's always a chance to bring the issue up later. It is the conspiracy of silence, the persistent avoidance of conflict, rather than conflict itself, that sabotages marriages.

Something else that's required for good communication is the willingness to listen to the other. Only half-jokingly, I have often said to groups of men, "You know, guys, the two most common complaints I hear from wives about their husbands are: First, they don't talk; and second, they don't listen!" The cartoon stereotype of the wife talking to the husband buried in the newspaper is, I'm afraid, an all-too-common reality. Or this classic scene:

Wife: "We need to talk."

Husband: "About what?"

Wife: "About you and me."

Husband: "Go ahead. I'm listening" (as he continues to stare at the TV screen).

Good listening, contrary to popular belief, does not come naturally. It is a discipline that requires practice and concentration. It requires, first of all, that we pay attention to the other. That means we lay aside, physically and mentally, what has been occupying us. It means we face the person and maintain eye contact with her. It means being willing to hear her out without interrupting. It means letting her know that we are "tracking" with her by an occasional nod of the head or facial expression. The simple act of paying attention to another is a wonderful way of saying, "You're important to me; I care about you and what you have to say." Unfortunately, it seems to be rare in our fast-paced society, which may explain why some people pay out substantial fees to have someone listen to them.

Good listening also involves trying not to make judgments about what is being said, to listen non-defensively. For instance, while the wife is talking, it is so tempting to dismiss what she says by passing it through our judgmental filters, like:

"She's on one of her kicks again."

"Sounds like her girlfriend has been filling her head with some more of her weird ideas."

"She sounds just like her mother."

"Why must women be so emotional?"

This is what prevents us from really hearing the other, and from responding in ways that will build intimacy. It would be much better if we could just relax and let the message come through. Even if we disagree, we can do so in a way that lets her know she has been understood: "O.K., I see what you're saying. You were upset because I seemed to side with our daughter against you. But let me tell you how I was seeing it. . . ." Besides preserving her self-esteem, this kind of listening and responding is the best basis for conflict resolution.

Earlier in this chapter we defined love as "the willingness to extend ourselves for the purpose of nurturing another's spiritual good."

Looking back, it is not hard to see that the kind of communication we have been describing is really a form of love. Self-disclosure, paying attention, non-judgmental listening and honest challenge are all acts of extending ourselves. They require effort and even entail risk. But they are all ways of nurturing the spouse's spiritual good (as well as our own), because they build up a sense of mutual reverence and care. Many couples have learned the skills and rewards of good communication by participating in a Marriage Encounter weekend.

The Power of Affirmation

But good communication is not the only way of showing love and creating communion. Another simple but powerful one is the act of affirming. This includes any word or action that builds up the spouse's sense of self-worth. Did you ever stop to think how little affirmation people experience in today's world? In our highly competitive society, we are preoccupied with keeping up with the competition and with winning. We hear plenty of criticism for our mistakes and inadequacies, but not very much by way of encouragement. If you are doing a good job, don't expect to be told about it because that's simply what's expected of you.

But most of us aren't made that way. I have heard a lot of men speak about this need for affirmation in their own lives. I know I need it myself. It encourages me to keep giving my best efforts; without it, I'm tempted to mediocrity and half-heartedness in my ministry. I know I should be more steady, more dedicated to working for the Lord than for human recognition, but I have not yet attained that level of purity of heart. Moreover, I know many men who thrive on a little affirmation from their bosses or co-workers. Any good book on management or human relations will tell you that.

What surprises me, though, is that so many men don't acknowledge that same need in their wives. One of the most frequent complaints I hear from wives is that they receive so little affirmation from their husbands. "While we were dating," they say, "he was so thoughtful and attentive. He would compliment me and let me know he appreciated little things I would do. But now, it seems, he just takes me for granted."

Part of this is natural, of course. Relationships, even intimate ones, tend to fall into routine patterns over time. But couples who do not make the effort to affirm one another over long periods of time are in danger of starving each other emotionally. Eventually it will mean the death of the relationship. I remember watching a television movie called *Superdome* some years ago. The star football player had become so engrossed with the game and with being a star that he was neglecting his wife and her needs. She began to blame herself for his apparent lack of interest and began consulting a psychiatrist. Some time later, in the midst of a heated quarrel with her husband, she blurted out, "I have to go out and pay a stranger money to tell me I'm still attractive!" Note well: The husband was not a bad man, and he really did love his wife. But, like too many others, he made the mistake of thinking that the big bucks and high prestige would make her happy. He didn't realize that all of it could not substitute for a little attention and honest caring.

Affirmation is such a simple action: an offer to help, a surprise note or phone call, a few words like:

"Thank you for taking care of that."

"I was really proud of you tonight."

"Today at work the guys were all griping about their wives, and I found myself thinking how lucky I am to have you."

Even teasing and playful "ribbing" about each other's little foibles can be fun forms of affirmation. But be careful here: If she's sensitive or embarrassed about something, keep it off-limits for teasing; it will only cause needless hurt. Also, if there is something that really annoys you about her, talk to her straight about it. If you try to use teasing to get your point across, you will only muddy the waters. As the communications people like to put it: "Say what you mean and mean what you say." Reminds me of the time I was greeting people after Sunday Mass. Quite a few made good comments on my homily for that day, but the one I remember best was by the guy who said, "You'd make a great used car salesman!" I'm still not sure if that was supposed to be a compliment or a put-down!

Sexual Love

I would not consider a discussion on the spirituality of love in marriage to be complete if I did not include some thoughts on sexual love. I can remember the days of the old-style parish mission where one of the nights would be devoted to a powerful sermon on sexual sins. After going through the expected list—masturbation, immodest dress, dirty books and movies, premarital sex—the preacher would say something like, "And now, if you married people think that single folks are the only ones who commit sexual sins, pay attention to this. . . ." Then would come the warnings on things like adultery, abortion and birth control.

I'm not suggesting that married people do not commit sexual sins. But I think we need to be more attentive to the subtler forms of such sins. But first, we need to focus on the positive Christian vision of marital sexuality. I recently taught an adult education class on "Christian Sexuality." I began by asking the participants (all of whom were laity): "From a purely human standpoint, what values should be present in any sexual activity?" Here are the answers they gave: mutual respect; love and care; trust; sensitivity to each other's needs; commitment; children. I was thrilled. With those values firmly in the center, it was easy to see why the familiar list of sexual sins are indeed departures from the divine plan for human sexuality: In one way or another, they negate or distort those deeper human values that "good sex" should embody.

Thankfully, the church today is trying to present a more positive vision of human sexuality. The Second Vatican Council expressed it in a way never before found in official church documents:

> Married love is uniquely expressed and perfected by the exercise of the acts proper to marriage. Hence the acts of marriage by which the intimate union of the spouses takes place are noble and honorable. The truly human performance of these acts fosters the self-giving they signify and enriches the spouses in joy and gratitude (*The Church in the Modern World*, n. 49).

A few years ago, Pope John Paul II devoted several months of his regular Wednesday audiences to profound reflections on the dignity of the human body and of married sexual love. He spoke often of the potential of sexual intercourse to bring the couple into deeper communion with God. These kinds of insights have been around in the church for a long time, but only in recent years are they being widely communicated. (John Paul's reflections on sexuality and marriage have been put together in a fine book entitled *Covenant Love*, by Richard Hogan and John LeVoir.)

Note, however, that it is not any and all kinds of sexual intercourse that fosters communion between the spouses and with God. The council speaks of "the truly human performance of these acts." That is, intercourse has to be an act of mutual love, not egoism.

"Truly human performance" means that the values we noted above (care, trust, mutual respect, sensitivity) must be preserved and enhanced. And here, I believe, is where sin can often creep in. When sex is demanded as a right, regardless of the other's condition or feelings; when it is denied as a form of punishment; when it is done hastily or without care and real passion; when it results in ridicule, humiliation, or put-down—sex loses its sacredness and its bonding power.

Sex is truly a language. It can speak either love or rejection, either self-gift or self-indulgence, either tenderness or violence. That is why it is so important for couples to talk to each other about their sex life. It has often been said that sex is not the be-all and end-all of marriage. True enough; but it is nevertheless a gauge, a barometer of the entire relationship. When something is out of kilter in the relationship, it will invariably affect sexual intimacy. Often, when couples start talking about their sex life, they find themselves moving into some other area of their relationship that really needs the attention, and then the sexual problem takes care of itself. Unfortunately, though, many couples are fearful of discussing sex because it can be a threat to their self-esteem. I have found time after time, however, that when there is genuine love between the two, an honest discussion of their sexual life has always led to healing and deepening of the relationship.

Forgiveness in Marriage

There is one final area of spirituality in marriage that we need to look at. It will be obvious by now that no couple will be able to practice the kind of love I have been describing in a perfectly consistent way. To reveal yourself to your spouse, to pay attention to her, to listen non-judgmentally, to challenge honestly, to give affirmation and to make sex a genuine expression of love—that is a lofty goal indeed. I am not saying it is unrealistic. But I am saying we must make allowances for human failure. And here is where another form of love comes into play: forgiveness. After all, the kind of love I am proposing to my male readers is also the norm for their wives. And they will not be able to carry it off perfectly, either. Which means that forgiveness will have to be a mutual attitude and action.

Again, here is where I have seen some otherwise good marriages suffer under great strain. One or the other spouse just will not forgive a past hurt. They keep hanging on to it and throwing it up to the other every time there is a quarrel. This kind of unforgiving attitude exacts a high price, however. While spouses hold grudges and wait for the other to make the first move, the walls between them grow higher and thicker. At the very least, low-level resentment, unexpressed and unresolved, gradually freezes out affection.

What finally brings most couples to forgiveness is the sheer pain that one or both spouses feel because of the strained relationship. It is the realization that their relationship is larger, deeper and more important than their quarrel. "Look," one of them says, "we've got too much going for us. Let's not blow it. Let's talk it out." But that takes humility. You have to swallow your pride and perhaps even apologize. You have to accept your spouse's imperfection, as well as your own.

I think God knew that forgiveness would not come easily for us. That's why we find it spoken of so often in the scriptures. In fact, in a couple of places in scripture we find that even God seems to have trouble forgiving. In the prophet Hosea, God appears to be arguing with himself about whether he should forgive his people for their infidelities. He reminds himself of how tenderly he started out loving them:

> It was I who taught [them] to walk,
>   I who took them in my arms;
> I drew them with human cords,
>   with bands of love (Hos 11:3-4).

But he is pained by their ingratitude and rejection; in fact, he is "tempted" to give up on them:

> Because they refused to repent,
>   their own counsels shall devour them. . . .
> And God, though in unison they
>   cry out to him, shall not raise them up
> (Hos 11:6-7).

But then we have to imagine a long pause in heaven, as if God has to really think about what he just said. Then, in a burst of compassion, God says,

> But how could I give you up . . . O Israel? . . .
> My heart is overwhelmed,
>   my pity is stirred.

> I will not give vent to my blazing anger. . . .
> For I am God and not man! (Hos 11:8-9).

What a touching, human picture. It reminds me of a dad who is ready to give up on his rebellious teenager, but just can't bring himself to do it. And I find it comforting to know that even God has to struggle with forgiveness.

When the Bible asks believers to forgive injuries, it gives only one reason: We ourselves have received forgiveness from God. The best way to show our gratitude is to "pass it on," to extend forgiveness to one another. As St. Paul puts it so beautifully: "Bearing with one another and forgiving one another, if one has a grievance against another; as the Lord has forgiven you, so must you also do" (Col 3:13). This does not mean that we have to condone the injury, or pretend that it did not hurt. Often it will take some time and arguing with ourselves before we're finally able to reach the point of forgiveness. Each couple, I have learned, works out their own little "rituals of forgiveness" as Dolores Curran calls them. One will say to the other, "Look, I feel stupid about what happened yesterday. I think I was right about one part of it, but I really wasn't listening to your side. Will you forgive me?" Or, "I know I was angry last night, but I really felt you took some cheap shots at me. Can we talk it out and put it behind us?" Some couples will use nonverbal signs of forgiveness, such as buying a gift or making love. This is fine, provided it doesn't just gloss over an issue which really needs to be talked through.

We began this chapter by saying that our quest for love is rooted in God's own plan for human fulfillment: We have a need to receive love as well as a call to give it. We looked at some of the attitudes and behaviors that constitute genuine love. And we reflected on some of the ways that the vocation to love is expressed in the special relationship of Christian marriage. I realize that the vision is not easy to attain. But this is why I like to remember the words of one of my favorite authors, G. K. Chesterton, who once said, "Whatever is worth doing, is worth doing poorly!" He purposely did not say "is worth doing well," because he wanted to emphasize the fact that if something is really worthwhile, then it should be done—even if we do it poorly. If we wait till we get it perfect, life will pass us by. God knows, I live my religious vows poorly. Most likely, you will live your marriage vows poorly, and love your children imperfectly and treat your friends carelessly—at least at times. But the vows are worth professing, and children are worth loving, and friends are worth being treated with care—imperfectly as we might do so. If we give it our best shot, I believe God will supply for our poverty and will graciously heal our mistakes.

BETTER TO DO
POORLY THAN
NOT DO ANY-
THING AT ALL

YOU CAN ALWAYS COR-
RECT MISTAKES (WELL
90% OF THE TIME).

6

A Man and His Responsibilities

When I was doing a lot of one-to-one counseling, I discovered that the process would usually follow a fairly predictable sequence. First I would spend a number of sessions mainly listening to the counselees. It was good for them to talk, to share with someone their pains, their hurts, their fears and their guilt. Sometimes I would ask questions that helped them to explore their experiences in a deeper and fuller way. At the same time, my attempts to listen and understand where they were coming from would build a "therapeutic alliance" between me and them, a trust and a bond that would be crucial for the harder work we had to do later.

Almost invariably, in this first stage of counseling, people would make statements like the following:

"My father and mother didn't love me, so I could never trust anyone."

"I get so angry at my wife because she spends money like there's no tomorrow."

"I left the church because I couldn't take all the garbage I saw going on in the parish."

"I got involved with this married man because my husband wasn't paying any attention to me."

You'll notice that every one of those statements makes sense. In each case the counselee's action seems understandable and even justifiable. We can almost hear ourselves saying, "Yeah, I don't blame you!"

But look a little more closely. Depending on the context and the tone of voice, every one of those statements can be seen as an evasion of responsibility. It's like the counselee is saying, "I had no choice but to do what I did. My attitudes and behavior are the inevitable result of what these other people have done to me." But isn't that unreasonable? Are there not other possible responses to parental rejection, bad spending habits, scandals in the parish, and an inattentive husband? So, in the second stage of counseling, I would have to begin challenging, gently but firmly, the counselee's failure to acknowledge responsibility for his or her choices. And this was always the crucial turning point. If the counselee would accept responsibility, we were free to explore other, more positive and healthy options. If not, I would be powerless to help.

I have been concerned about this issue for a long time, because it seems to me that irresponsibility is a growing problem in today's society. Too many people want to put the blame for their unhappiness on other people, or expect other people to do something to make them happy. We seem to have lost the sense that we are the ones who have the power, by the choices we make, either to find or to miss happiness.

Psychiatrists and other therapists have been saying that they are seeing more and more people who are not mentally or emotionally ill in the usual sense, but who have serious "character disorders"—self-centered, irresponsible patterns of thinking and acting. Social critic Christopher Lasch in his book *The Culture of Narcissism* claims that our society is spawning an unprecedented number of narcissistic personalities—people who live primarily for their own self-gratification. Superficially charming and likable, they easily talk their way into the right social and business circles. When they fail to follow through on their responsibilities, as they often do, they are skilled at making plausible-sounding excuses and thus manage to avoid damaging criticism. They appear to make friends easily, but their relationships are never deep or lasting. Lasch quotes one man who said to his therapist, "The ideal relationship for me would be two months. That way there'd be no commitment. At the end of two months I'd just break it off." We Americans keep saying we want to be bonded to our families and other social communities, but we are unwilling to give up any of our individual freedom to make that happen. We resist the notion that we are accountable to, or responsible for, anyone besides ourselves.

Responsibility in Scripture

Christians have always struggled with this issue of personal responsibility. We are profoundly aware of the forces that can pull us away from the holiness and integrity to which God calls us. The strength of our own desires for self-indulgence ("original sin") plus the false values and appeals of the society around us ("the sin of the world") often combine to pressure us away from our commitment to a truly spiritual life. Again, the first pages of the Bible show us clearly that we ourselves have to bear the responsibility for our choices. God did not allow Adam and Eve to project blame upon each other or the serpent for their sin. Later, when God found Cain indulging in a bout of self-pity, he told him, "If you do well, you can hold up your head; but if not, sin is a demon lurking at your door. His urge is toward you, yet you can be his master" (Gn 4:7). Later, when Cain had murdered Abel, God would not let him dodge responsibility by claiming he is not his brother's keeper. This doctrine of personal freedom and responsibility is summed up very strikingly in the book of Sirach:

> When God, in the beginning, created man,
> he made him subject to his own free choice.
> If you choose you can keep the commandments;
> it is loyalty to do his will.
> There are set before you fire and water;
> to whichever you choose, stretch forth your hand.
> Before man are life and death;
> whichever he chooses shall be given him. . . .
> The eyes of God see all he has made,
> he understands man's every deed.
> No one does he command to sin (Sir 15:14-17, 19-20).

I have always been puzzled by people who talk as though human beings had no real freedom, that we are tossed about helplessly on the sea of life. I suppose it is comforting to think that our mistakes and sins are not really our own fault, that it is all a matter of how we are programmed by family or society. But if that is true, then why make a fuss over people who make wise, honorable, or heroic choices? For if no one deserves blame, then no one deserves praise either.

One of the books that had a deep impact on me was *Man's Search for Meaning*, by psychiatrist Viktor Frankl. He begins with his experiences of being a prisoner in a Nazi concentration camp during World War II. As he observed the horrors and indignities inflicted on his fellow prisoners, he noted that many of them became nearly as callous and inhuman as their guards; others simply gave up hope and died. But some of them managed to rise above the terrible conditions of their environment; as Frankl says, they were able to find some sense of meaning or purpose there. For some, it was the fact that family members were counting on them to survive; for others, it was to show the Nazis that they could not be broken; still others were able to find a religious meaning in their suffering, linking them with the suffering of Christ for the redemption of the world. Reflecting on this, Frankl says:

> We who lived in concentration camps can remember the men who walked through the huts comforting others, giving away their last piece of bread. They may have been few in number, but they offer sufficient proof that everything can be taken from a man but one thing—the last of the human freedoms: to choose one's attitude in any given set of circumstances, to choose one's own way.

Isn't that the truth? Sometimes the only freedom we have is the ability to choose our own inner attitude. But that choice can have profound consequences for our behavior: We will become either more loving or less loving, peaceful or resentful, thoughtful of others or self-centered, hopeful or bitter.

This whole matter of finding a meaning and choosing one's attitude became key concepts for Frankl. He recalled the words of the philosopher Nietzsche, "He who has a *why* to live can bear with almost any *how*." Frankl found that one of the greatest dangers in the concentration camp was despair. The typical statement of the prisoner who had given up the quest for meaning was, "There is nothing more to expect from life." But Frankl turns the whole argument around:

> What was really needed was a fundamental change in our attitude toward life. We had to learn ourselves and, furthermore, we had to teach the despairing men, that it did not really matter what we expected from life, but rather what life expected from us. We needed to stop asking about the meaning of life, and instead to think of ourselves as those who were being questioned by life—daily and hourly. Our answer must consist, not in talk and meditation, but in right action and in right conduct. Life ultimately means taking the responsibility to find the right answer to its problems and to fulfill the tasks which it constantly sets for each individual.

"It is we who are questioned by life." Or, as we saw in the first chapter, it is really God who questions us, and we are called to answer. That is what it means to be responsible, "capable of responding," and not only blindly and instinctively like the animals, but freely. We alone have the freedom not to respond, and even to respond badly.

After Frankl was freed from prison and went back to his psychiatric practice, he began to see that many of the problems people were bringing to his office were ultimately spiritual problems—questions of meaning and responsibility. So he developed a new form of treatment which he called "logotherapy," in which he tried to help people to take responsibility for their attitudes and their actions, and to change them if necessary. This is very close to the way we have been looking at spirituality as "vision and lifestyle"—a way of seeing reality in the light of God's truth and making choices accordingly.

So a Christian who is striving to lead a spiritual life will be very conscious of this whole matter of responsibility. We have to be careful here, though, not to think of responsibility as another burden laid on us by a grumpy God or by scowling clerics. We need to remember all that we said in the first chapter about the very first movement of spirituality—namely, that God takes the initiative. He reaches out to us, knocks on the door of our heart, not to threaten or burden us, but to be our friend. He wants to share his own divine life with us and to make sure we do not miss the happiness for which he created us. And one of the great signs of his confidence in us, I think, is the fact that he has entrusted the care of the world to us.

Let's look a little more closely at this. One of the biblical truths that has nourished me greatly is that God has confidence in me. It took me a long time to realize that, because I had to struggle a lot with lack of self-confidence. I remember how moved I was the first time I heard the "Credo" from Leonard Bernstein's Mass. The young singer begins by saying how difficult it is for him to say "Credo" ("I believe"). Then he proceeds to sing:

> I'll believe in God, if he'll believe in me.
> I'll believe in thirty gods, if they'll believe in me.
> I'll believe in sugar and spice, and everything nice,
> I'll believe in you, and you, and you—
> But who—yes who—will believe in me?

Isn't that the cry of the human heart? We all need someone who believes in us, who sees some good in us, some potential that can be activated. As I read the scriptures more carefully, I came to realize that God is telling us he really does have confidence in us—and I found that to be good news.

In Chapter 4 we saw how God has given his human creatures "dominion" over all the works of creation and that this gives a divine significance to human work. We are called to use our knowledge and our skills to develop our universe according to God's plan, so that its resources will benefit all of life. God has made us responsible for the earth, "to cultivate and care for it" (Gn 2:15). That shows a great deal of confidence in us on the part of God. That's why it is so tragic when we abuse our dominion of the earth—when we slaughter the buffalo herds, destroy the great rain forests (which preserve our very oxygen supply), pollute our lakes and streams, and use nuclear power to manufacture deadly weapons. Surely these are betrayals of God's trust in us.

We also saw, in Chapter 5, that we are responsible for one another. God has called us above all to care for one another in love, which we defined as "extending ourselves for the purpose of nurturing another's spiritual growth." We spent some time reflecting on the special kind of love required for happy marriages. Now we want to take a look at the issue of responsibility in marriage.

Responsibility in Marriage

In my 20-plus years of counseling with individuals and married couples, I have become increasingly concerned about the irresponsibility I see in so many married men. I'm not saying I don't see it also in women, but I would have to say that I have found it more frequently in the male of the species. My impressions are confirmed by my reading and my conversations with other professionals. One has to wonder: What is our society doing (or not doing) to young males that seems to predispose them toward remaining boys instead of growing up to be responsible men? We discussed some possibilities in Chapter 2, when we looked at the issue of male self-esteem. Much more could be said about this, but I want to move on to describe the phenomenon more fully.

What I have seen so often is a husband who never really made the transition from single life to married life. He continued the pattern of spending his nights and Saturdays with "the guys." When he was home, he insisted on having everything his way. If he got involved with the children at all, it was to order them around and make sure they did not disturb his routines, especially his television. But he expected his wife to manage the house, pay the bills and take care of the children's needs. She was his playmate and sex partner, but he could not see her as a person with needs of her own for genuine love and affection, much less as his equal. If she began to make even minimal demands on him, he would find ways to retaliate. In such a marriage, it was not hard to predict that adultery would enter the picture sooner or later. For him, it was a way of having sex with no other demands; for the wife, it was a way to feel loved and cared for. The scenarios varied, of course, but the basic patterns were predictable. The common theme was: These men could not accept the fact that a marriage relationship is something that has to be worked at. It requires some degree of self-investment and self-sacrifice, something which they could not or would not put forth.

One variation on the theme is the man who starts out really trying to invest himself in the relationship; but then, when he discovers that it requires continuous effort, he backs off. This is one of the things that can happen when a man reaches midlife. He grows tired of adult responsibilities and tries to recapture the carefree days of youth. To others it looks like a complete personality change. He drives faster, drinks more, dresses like his kids, stops going to church, spends money with abandon. He may even quit his job. He may start flirting and looking for sex with younger women. And he will rationalize his behavior by saying, "I'm tired of being a good soldier. It's time I started to enjoy life." Sometimes these men can be helped through this period by relatively brief counseling with someone who understands midlife transition.

But let's take a closer look at some of the more common forms of irresponsibility. I once read a fascinating book by Clayton Barbeau called *Delivering the Male*. The title itself was interesting, and so was the subtitle: "Out of the Tough-Guy Trap into a Better Marriage." A marriage counselor himself, his experiences were similar to my own. He too believes that the cultural conditioning many men receive does not prepare them well for marriage. In particular, the overemphasis on independence, on competition, on winning, on being in control make it difficult for many men to really blend their lives with another person. He finds that the chief complaint of wives is that their men are not grown-up. This seems to take one of two forms: Either the man is a dictator, demanding that everyone conform to his expectations; or he acts like a little boy, avoiding responsibility and demanding that his wife take care of him like a mother.

In the first case, Barbeau says, the man may seek to wield power over "the little woman" and the kids because he feels powerless at work. His job may be dull and routine, or he feels he has no control over his work environment. So he thinks he has to be "in charge" at home in order to feel like a strong male. Such men are threatened even if someone in the family expresses an opinion different from theirs. Barbeau says:

> By their mistaken belief that "authority" over their children is something they can arbitrarily impose, that "respect" is something that they can demand, that manly strength is measured only in terms of the visible submission of others to their will, they alienate their wives and children and destroy the foundations of family life.

Ironically, but not surprisingly, these strong-arm methods backfire. Instead of becoming submissive, his children turn rebellious. They take drugs, become pregnant, run away from home, or move out as soon as possible. His wife spends more and more time working or being with friends. And sadly, the man wonders why no one appreciates all the material things he has worked so hard to provide.

The second type of irresponsible male described by Barbeau is the one who expects to be taken care of by his wife without giving very much in return. We have all seen marriages like this which seem to "work" well enough, because the husband's wish to be taken care of is matched by the wife's need to be a caretaker. But more and more women are refusing to be thrust into that role. They want a man who will be a partner and a companion, not another child. They want a man who will not pout when they happen to disagree with him, will not explode when they can't always be there for him, will not have to spend half their time soothing his bruised ego.

The "real men" who have inspired me to write this book are those who have risen above the desire to dominate as well as the wish to remain boys. They are striving, not without some failures, to be responsible husbands. They are sharing with their wives the tasks of maintaining a home, caring for children and meeting each other's needs. And they are finding this to be more satisfying and rewarding than neglect or avoidance of responsibility. Which brings me to my next point.

Avoidance of Problems

One common form of irresponsibility that I have seen is the man who simply will not deal with problems. The classic example, of course, is alcoholism. Even in this enlightened age, when alcoholism is regarded more as an illness which is treatable than as a moral failure, some men will go on for years denying that they have a problem with alcohol. We have all heard the standard lines: "I've never missed a day of work because of drinking" (he neglects to mention the fact that he's bombed out every weekend). "I haven't had a drink for six weeks" (he doesn't tell you he's done that a dozen times before and always slips back). "My buddies drink a lot more than I do" (which may be true but has nothing to do with *his* addiction). I wish everyone could sit in on a retreat for recovering alcoholics and listen to the miracles of grace that happened when they finally admitted their problem and began seeking help.

Another example: Why do men as a group have more health problems and die at an earlier age than women? Part of the reason, I'm sure, is the work-related stress that men are under. Part of it, as I said in the last chapter, is the difficulty men have in disclosing themselves and talking about their problems. But another reason is that men tend to deny their symptoms. For one thing, it's not macho to be sick. Besides, it's scary to think about what the doctors might find out. So good old denial wins again. I sometimes get very angry at society for making it so difficult for men who are hurting—physically, emotionally, or spiritually—to simply go to a fellow human being and say, "I'm sick. I need help."

Avoidance and denial can creep into so many areas of life. A man will be miserable on the job: He will complain to his wife and to anyone else who will listen, but he will not talk to his supervisor or anyone else who could do something about it. Why?—because he's afraid he will lose face, or he will be looked upon as a troublemaker. So often it is fear that is the real enemy. The marriage relationship shows clear signs of deteriorating, but neither spouse will talk about it because it could be too painful. Meanwhile, the poison continues to spread until it is too late. I can't tell you how often, after listening to a couple express the hopelessness of their relationship, I found myself saying, "If only they had come a year ago, or even six months ago, I could have helped them." And, as I mentioned in an earlier chapter, I don't know how many times a husband won't come because "we don't have any problems we can't solve ourselves." There's a good example of denial feeding on the macho image. When it's the case of a child showing behavior problems, both parents may work out a conspiracy of denial. But again, my experience is that the father more often than the mother will tend to ignore it or to play it down as nothing more than "growing pains."

I have a good deal of sympathy for men like this. I myself tend to let things ride in the belief that they will work themselves out. But sometimes I know this approach is just an excuse for laziness or cowardice on my part. It has helped me to recall that one of the great Christian virtues is courage (the old word for it was "fortitude," remember?). One of the finest ways for a man to develop "manliness" is to exercise courage. I think this means being willing to face and overcome life's problems rather than try to escape from them. There is that human tendency toward escape, and we are living in a culture that reinforces it. Day in and day out we drink in the message that life is supposed to be problem-free and painless. We are encouraged to "go for it," told that we can "have it all." Our technology provides us with instant gratification of our wants. The purpose of life is to consume and enjoy, is it not? In such a world-view, problems are nothing but a nuisance. Yet, it is in the very process of meeting and solving problems that life takes on meaning and that we grow mentally and spiritually.

I have seen that truth many times, both in my own life and in that of others. Taking responsibility for solving our problems is the surest way to strengthen our self-esteem and to overcome our sense of powerlessness. As children we felt good about ourselves when a grown-up showed an interest in us and spent time with us. Later, it was making friends and doing well in sports or school projects that built our self-esteem. As adults we tend to measure our worth by the symbols of success—money, possessions, occupational status. There is nothing wrong with any of this. But it will not be enough unless we also have the satisfaction of knowing that we tried our best to solve the problems that life thrust upon us.

This is where I find it helpful to reflect on the life of Jesus. He had a lot of success the first year or so of his public life. His teaching sessions drew huge crowds. He expelled demonic spirits and healed people with terminal diseases. Life-long sinners broke with their past and turned back to God. But Jesus knew it would not last. Eventually he would have to face rejection and finally the cross. Halfway through his gospel account, Luke sets us up for the turning point when he writes: "As the time approached when Jesus was to be taken from this world, he firmly resolved to proceed toward Jerusalem" (Lk 9:51). "He firmly resolved to proceed." What a strong image of courage, of facing life's problems rather than running from them. Three times Jesus tried to tell the disciples that they had to be ready for trouble, that he himself will have to undergo suffering and death. But each time the disciples resorted to denial (Mk 8:31-33; 9:30-32; 10:32-45). Jesus would not back down. In fact, he let the disciples know that they could not really be his followers unless they were willing to take up their cross each day—that is, to face and deal with the conflicts, challenges and problems of their own lives as Christians. This is another way of saying that the Christian life is a life of responsibility.

At the same time, Jesus knew that this would be hard on our human nature. So he assured his disciples that he would not leave them to struggle alone. At the Last Supper he told them,

> "In this world you will have trouble,
> but take courage,
> I have conquered the world" (Jn 16:33).

He promised to send them the Holy Spirit, who would give them the power and the wisdom to overcome the problems they would have to face. Christ has made that same commitment to us. We are his disciples today, and we have received the Holy Spirit in our baptism and confirmation. We can count on him to help us in our efforts to be responsible Christians. One of St. Paul's letters was written to his young friend Timothy, whom Paul had appointed to be the bishop of Ephesus. Timothy was not very sure of himself, but Paul had confidence in him and kept encouraging him. In one place he reminds him to trust in the power of the Holy Spirit more than in himself: "The Spirit which God has given us is no cowardly spirit, but rather one that makes us strong, loving and wise. Therefore . . . with the strength which comes from God, bear your share of the hardship which the gospel entails" (2 Tm 1:7-8). The Christian life is never an easy escape into pious longing for the next life, but a courageous taking of responsibility for the betterment of ourselves, our loved ones and our world.

Authority in Marriage

Married couples who are spiritually mature will find themselves working together to deal with their problems. And they share their authority rather than fight about "who's in charge." This may be as good a place as any to tackle that old question about who is the rightful "head of the family." It is often said that St. Paul made it perfectly clear when he wrote, "Wives should be subordinate to their husbands as to the Lord" (Eph 5:22). But a closer reading of the whole section can lead us to a more careful interpretation. After all, Paul could not possibly mean that wives should obey even when husbands are unreasonable.

The key, I think, is in the verse just before, where Paul is talking to the whole Christian community and says, "Be subordinate to one another out of reverence for Christ" (Eph 5:21). Jesus himself had often warned the apostles not to exercise power and domination over one another like the pagans do: "Just so, the Son of Man did not come to be served but to serve and to give his life as a ransom for many" (Mt 20:28). So Paul is reminding all Christians that they must not get bogged down in power struggles among themselves. If everyone keeps demanding his or her own way, nothing will get done; the kingdom of God will be held back rather than built up. The body of Christ will suffer from internal divisions. Hurt will replace love. The remedy, Paul says, is to defer to one another—that is, be willing to sacrifice some of your wants or preferences for the sake of unity in the body of Christ.

In the verses which follow, Paul is simply applying this principle to Christian marriage. Wives and husbands must both learn to defer or yield to one another "out of reverence for Christ"—that is, out of regard for the covenant, the sacramental bond in Christ that is the heart of their marriage. So when Paul says, "Wives, be subordinate to your husbands as to the Lord," he is saying, "Be willing at times to sacrifice some of your will, your freedom, for the sake of strengthening the marriage relationship." He implies that the deference is to be mutual when he adds, "Husbands, love your wives as Christ loved the church [and] gave himself up for her" (Eph 5:25). That is, "Be willing at times to sacrifice some of your own comfort, will or interests for the sake of strengthening the marriage bond." This is a profound view of marriage, because it sees Christ as the center; it is he who has authority, even over the individual wills of the partners. But it is also a view that is strongly countercultural, in an age when the culture exalts individuality and personal autonomy. The Christian vision calls for a willingness to yield some individuality and autonomy for the sake of building the marriage relationship.

There can be problems here, of course. The main danger is that one of the spouses will defer so much to the other "for the sake of peace" that the marriage will end up being a dominance-submission relationship. The obvious extreme would be spouse abuse. But there are more subtle forms as when one spouse becomes overly compliant, never stands up for his or her rights, or becomes a doormat for the other. This is certainly not what Paul had in mind in Ephesians 5. His basic assumption was that Christian spouses believed in their mutual dignity and equality, as he had written (and preached) earlier:

> For through faith you are all children of God in Christ Jesus.
> For all of you who were baptized into Christ have clothed yourselves with Christ. There is neither Jew nor Greek, there is not male and female; for you are all one in Christ Jesus (Gal 3:26-28).

It is not that baptism has wiped out all differences between people; we still retain our uniqueness and individuality. But baptism removes all reasons for separateness or inequality based on mere cultural prejudices. Christian marriage was calling for husbands and wives to form a new kind of partnership. While reverencing each other's uniqueness and freedom, they were to blend their lives in a deeper unity in Jesus Christ, always putting him at the center and asking, "What is the Lord asking of us? What is the loving way to act in this situation?" This has to imply, I think, that couples are praying together. I want to say more about that in the next chapter.

Before I leave the topic of responsibility in marriage, I would like to suggest that when a couple does learn to exercise mutuality in caring for one another and in decision making, they will become a source of healing for one another. They will confirm each other's sense of self-worth. They will strengthen each other in their low

times. And they will gain a sense of power and competence from experiencing themselves as capable of solving their problems together.
All of that is surely at the heart of God's plan for marriage.

Responsibility for Children

Now let's turn to another kind of love and responsibility—
caring for children. Let's begin with the fact that every research
study ever conducted on families has shown the importance of the
father in normal development of children. The exact nature of this
influence, and how it differs from the mother's, is not yet clear. But
the more I read and the more I listen to people, the more convinced I
am that God is very wise in providing that children be raised by two
parents. It is sometimes said that the father is the one who confers
sexual identity on the child: He models masculinity for his sons and
affirms his daughters' femininity by the way he treats them and their
mother. I'm not sure of this, but it makes some sense to me. I know
that children can be brought up well in one-parent families, but it is
always difficult.

What do children need from their dads? For one thing, time and
attention. A psychologist whose name I've forgotten once said, "How
do we build children's self-esteem? My answer is so simple that you'll
be tempted not to believe it: Spend time with them." I believe that;
when I freely spend time with someone, it's a clear sign that I think
he or she is worthwhile. One of the problems of our modern era is
that fathers often don't seem to have time for their children. James
Dobson, in his book *What Wives Wish Their Husbands Knew About
Women*, cites a study that showed that middle-class fathers inter-
acted directly with their small children an average of only a few minutes a day.

I can imagine it would be hard for a man to come home after
working all day at a job that involved talking with adults, often
about highly technical matters, and then have to listen to the seemingly trivial chatter of young children. But dads who neglect to do
that simple action will miss precious opportunities to build their
child's self-esteem. I have been a spiritual director to a great number of people. I wish you could hear the tone of voice and see the
look of appreciation in the faces of men and women when they tell
me how their dad used to take them for walks and showed them the
beauties of nature; or played games with them, or told them stories

about "the olden days," or just read to them. By contrast, I have listened to too many counselees tell me, with deep pain, how much they missed all this: "Dad was never around; or if he was, he was always too tired."

Fathers who are willing to spend time with their children usually find that it not only helps the child's self-esteem—it also gives Dad a deep feeling of satisfaction. For the "trivial chatter" of children gradually becomes more interesting, more inquiring, more challenging. Fathers have told me that getting involved with their kids has kept them feeling young and made them want to keep learning new things. There is a reciprocity, a happy spillover effect that benefits both.

Here I would like to say a special word to fathers of daughters. Sometimes dads have a tendency to pull away when their daughters reach puberty. Particularly if they have had an affectionate relationship with their daughters, fathers may be concerned about sexual stimulation. There certainly is need for caution here, especially since we know there have been so many cases of father-daughter incest. But, assuming that this is not the case, fathers should beware of abruptly withdrawing affection from their adolescent daughters. The girl can too easily interpret this as rejection, particularly of her sexuality, which can complicate her psychosexual development. The father may indeed have to modify his relationship with his daughter at this point. But even if he is less physical with her, she still needs an occasional hug from him and a general sense that he approves of her growing femininity.

Besides building self-esteem, spending time with children is a simple but effective way of communicating values to them. So many parents I talk with nowadays are deeply concerned about this. In contrast to previous generations, today's children are exposed to value messages from all kinds of sources other than their parents. The research tells us that young children watch at least 30 hours of television per week (compare that with the average few minutes a day that their fathers spend with them). Later on the world of rock music, movies and the pressures of the peer group will have a powerful shaping influence. The public schools have long ago opted out of the values arena, leaving a vacuum that will readily be filled by other forces. So parents who cherish their own values will have to make good use of the opportunities they do have to communicate values to their children.

For one thing, children need regular exposure to clear value messages. They need to hear parents say things like:

"In this family we expect thus-and-so."

"We don't talk that way in this home."

"We don't believe in that kind of thing."

"This is important to us because we're Christians."

Young children will absorb value messages almost by osmosis. With older children, however, parents will have to be ready to give some reasons for their value positions.

These verbal messages, moreover, have to be reinforced by good modeling on the part of parents. If children see that their parents contradict what they say (by lying, cheating, cutting others down, drinking too much, etc.), the verbal messages will be held in contempt. The same will happen if parents are inconsistent about what they approve or disapprove. Children will get the message: "What they say is less important than the mood they're in." Speaking of moods, one of the surest ways for parents to discredit their own values is to give the impression that following them is a grim and gloomy business. That is, if parents are always tired or crabby or too busy to enjoy the present moment, kids will draw the conclusion that virtue is a drag. Children need to see that parents are happy about their values. Especially later on, when they hear their parents' values ridiculed, they will recall that Mom and Dad were not only good people but happy people.

One other thing about values. Even if they are put forth clearly and consistently and accompanied by positive modeling, children will seldom appropriate them without first testing them. The child can't help wondering, "What will happen if I defy my parents' expectations?" This is why rules need to be backed up by sanctions. And here it is important to recognize that yelling, cursing, name-calling and tearful hand-wringing are not sanctions. They may "work" the first few times, but children quickly get used to them, especially when they see that nothing further happens except that Mom and Dad get upset. Effective sanctions are those that have an impact on the child, not the parents. That is why wise parents learn, without losing their cool, to do something like impose extra work, deny privileges (no TV, no snacks, no leaving the house), or cut the child's allowance.

What we are talking about here is discipline. I find that a lot of fathers are all too willing to abdicate their responsibility here and leave it up to their wives. Sometimes it's out of a desire to play the role of Big Daddy or Mr. Nice Guy for their children. Sometimes it's just plain laziness, not wanting to put forth the effort it takes to exercise discipline. But that really isn't fair to the wife. She ends up with all the unpleasant stuff, while Dad is the one who hands out the goodies. Not only that, but it backfires in the end. Children need to experience a father's firmness as well as his gentleness. Otherwise, they will secretly begin to regard him as a wimp. They will feel let down, because they know (at a pre-conscious level) that good discipline is a form of love. That's why it says in the scriptures:

> He who loves his son chastises him often,
>   that he may be his joy when he grows up.

And:

> He who spoils his son will have wounds to bandage (Sir 30:1,7).

For further insights on this subject, I would recommend another fine book by Dr. James Dobson: *Dare to Discipline*.

Working for a Better World

There is one other area of responsibility that I would like to talk about. I think most people can see, at least intellectually, that they have a responsibility to do a good job at work, to create a good marriage, and to care for their children. And most Christians, recalling the parable of the Good Samaritan, would agree that they also have a responsibility to help another human being who is in obvious need. But some people would bristle at the suggestion that God has given us a further responsibility—that of building a better world, a better human community. "Why should I?" they ask. "That's the job of politicians and statesmen. That's what we pay them for." Even people with strong religious convictions may sincerely wonder about this. They say, "I pray. I go to church regularly. I help my neighbor in need. What more do you want?"

Let me start with a personal experience. Recently I watched the PBS television series called "Eyes on the Prize." It was a powerful documentary on the early struggle for civil rights in the South in the late 1950s and early 1960s. We saw the television film clips of the Montgomery bus boycott, the freedom rides and marches, the lunch counter sit-ins, the speeches of Dr. Martin Luther King and other black leaders. We even saw the brutal attacks on the peaceful demonstrators by armed policemen and vicious dogs. As I was watching I asked myself, "Where was I through all this? How did I miss it?" I knew I was busy trying to keep up with graduate studies in psychology. And our Order didn't allow us to watch TV at that time. But I was appalled by my ignorance of this part of history. Another question kept bugging me as I was watching the series: "Where was the church?" The Baptist churches were the spiritual backbone of the civil rights movement. Other Protestant ministers soon got involved, but it was quite a while later before Catholic priests, nuns and laity joined the struggle. I still remember a couple of Catholic graduate students I was studying with coming to me with a lot of concern because they didn't see the church involved in one of the major issues of the time. The same criticism was heard, as you recall, during the Vietnam War.

I suppose it could be said that the church was preoccupied with its own internal affairs at the time: The Second Vatican Council was in its first phases. But the bishops at the council were very much aware of the issues, especially as they listened to the struggles of people in Asia, Africa, Latin America and elsewhere. So when the documents were finally produced by the council, they contained clear teachings on the necessity for all members of the church to work for the building of a more just and peaceful world. For example:

> It is a mistake to think that, because we have here no lasting city but seek the city which is to come, we are therefore entitled to shirk our earthly responsibilities. . . . But it is no less mistaken to think that we may immerse ourselves in earthly activities as if these latter were utterly foreign to religion, and religion were nothing more than the fulfillment of acts of worship and the observance of a few moral obligations (*The Church in the Modern World*, no. 43).

Note how careful the bishops are not to split our spiritual life from our temporal life—the very point we have been trying to make throughout this book. Later in that same text they say very forcefully that there must be "no opposition between professional and social activity on the one hand and religious life on the other. The Christian who shirks his temporal duties shirks his duties toward his neighbor, neglects God himself, and endangers his eternal salvation." Those are strong words indeed. Moreover, in their great *Dogmatic Constitution on the Church*, the bishops devote a whole chapter to the role of the laity. The "special vocation" of the laity, they say, "is to seek the kingdom of God by engaging in temporal concerns and directing them according to God's will" (no. 31). They encourage lay Christians to develop their skills in the secular disciplines so that the good things of God's creation may serve the needs of all people on earth, not just the privileged few. When they find that certain institutions or social arrangements have become unjust, they are to seek out ways to reform them "that these may be conformed to the norms of justice" (n. 36).

So the council gave out a clear call to all Catholics to lend their energies to the building of a just human world. But it was only the beginning. As the agitations of the 1960s accelerated, people everywhere were confronted with the harsh realities of poverty, hunger, tortures and political imprisonments, terrorism, and demeaning forms of oppression and discrimination. And the church, led by Pope Paul VI, became more bold in speaking out. In every one of his major addresses, the pope denounced injustice, violence and oppression wherever he saw it. In 1971 he called the bishops of the world together for a synod on "Justice in the World." After prayer and reflection together, they issued a strong prophetic document in which they declared that the preaching of the gospel must include "action on behalf of justice and participation in the transformation of the world." Pope John Paul II has continued speaking out forcefully against every system or institution that stifles human freedom and dignity. He will go down in history, I believe, as one of the great champions of the dignity and fundamental rights of the human person.

So the church's teaching is clear. But how is the average Catholic layman supposed to respond to all this? I think the first response ought to take the form of education. We Catholics have inherited a rich tradition of teaching on social issues that is rooted in the scriptures and goes back to the earliest days of the church. Just to take one example, the letter of James denounces those Christians who try to discriminate against the poor:

> My brothers, show no partiality as you adhere to the faith in our glorious Lord Jesus Christ. For if a man with gold rings comes into your assembly, and a poor person in shabby clothes also comes in, and you pay attention to the one wearing the fine

clothes and say, "Sit here, please," while you say to the poor
one, "Stand there," or "Sit at my feet," have you not made dis-
tinctions among yourselves and become judges with evil de-
signs? (Jas 2:1-4).

Then James goes on to challenge those who have grown rich by not
paying decent wages to their laborers (5:1-6).

In our own day, our American bishops have struggled long and
hard with contemporary moral issues such as abortion, pornography, family life and education. Their most recent documents, *The
Challenge of Peace* (1983) and *Economic Justice for All* (1986), are
intended to give us moral guidance on two of the most urgent issues of
our time: nuclear war and the economy. The least we can do is to
familiarize ourselves with these teachings.

When we take the time and effort to educate ourselves, we will
be led to respond in other ways as well. We Americans have a deeply
ingrained sense of fairness, probably based on our democratic ideals.
So, when we are faced with instances of injustice or unfairness, our
minds are quick to judge, "That isn't right!" Let's make this very specific and concrete:

• It is not right that over one million human lives are aborted
every year in this country.

• It is not right that in this land of abundance, 33 million people still live in poverty, and that poverty is increasing in this country
rather than decreasing. "For a people who believe in 'progress,' this
should be cause for alarm," the U.S. bishops say.

• It is not right that there are eight million people in the United
States who are looking for a job but cannot find one.

• It is not right that there are still thousands of hungry and
homeless people in this great land of ours, and over 400 million people on our planet who are undernourished or actually starving.

• It is not right that women and members of racial minorities
receive unequal treatment in this country that boasts of its freedom
and equal opportunity for all.

• It is not right that the Pentagon spends over one billion dollars every working day, while so many human services are being cut
off.

Once we make the judgment that "It is not right," where do we
go from there? Do we shrug our shoulders and say, "Well, these
problems are so enormous—I can't do anything about them"? No,

that wouldn't be right for a Christian who is trying to grow in the spiritual life. More and more Christians are saying, "Maybe I don't have final answers to these problems, but I can at least make a start. Jesus asked us to 'hunger and thirst for justice' (Mt 5:6); I can at least do that. And that may lead me to some kind of action, either on my own or joined with other people."

Let me say a word here about one response that would be inappropriate. I'm talking about guilt. If one has worked hard and managed to improve one's standard of living, there is no need to feel guilty. The right question here is: Do I care about those who are still in need? Our society has ways of teaching us to be insensitive to the injustices and sufferings of the disadvantaged. Television would rather show us "The Lifestyles of the Rich and Famous," rather than "The Plight of the Poor." Back in the fourth century, St. John Chrysostom saw that the Christians of his time were becoming comfortable because they were no longer a persecuted minority; in the process, they were neglecting the poor in their midst. So in one of his sermons he challenged them: "How can you clothe the body of Christ on the altar with silver and gold, but ignore the body of Christ starving in the streets?" He did not ask them to renounce their possessions or their status, but to use their influence to make sure that the poor were properly cared for.

Let me now cite some examples of what Christians are doing to respond to the call to build peace and justice. The place to begin is always in our own hearts. We need to scrutinize our own attitudes and assumptions, and then humbly ask the Lord to correct them or root them out if they are contrary to the Christian vision. For instance, do I really believe in the dignity and equality of every human being, regardless of race or sex? How do I talk about Blacks, Hispanics, or Indians? Am I willing to challenge the guys when they are belittling women or making them over into mere sex objects? Do I really believe that pornography is an exploitation of human beings rather than a harmless pastime? Are there still traces of violence in me, however subtle they may be? This honest self-examination is something that needs to continue all through our lifetime.

Those of you who are parents have an important mission to help form your children in correct attitudes based on human dignity. Just the way you talk about the poor, about racial minorities and about women will have a powerful effect on your children. Not long ago

Cardinal Joseph Bernardin of Chicago wrote a very thoughtful column in the archdiocesan paper entitled "Sexism is the Enemy." He started with a story of a five-year-old boy who one day announced to his mother (a full-time homemaker, mother of six and active in her husband's business), "Mom, you're lucky; you don't have to work!" Fortunately, his Dad took the occasion to carefully explain to him that raising children, keeping up a home and sharing the toil of a new business venture qualified as work—hard work. But the Cardinal pointed out the rather tragic fact that already by age five, this boy had grasped one of our society's wrong notions: What is valuable is rewarded with money, and that somehow our societal structures regard women as less valuable than men. If you would like some further help in ways that Christian parents can offset the negative messages of our culture, I would recommend a book by James and Kathleen McGinnis entitled *Parenting for Peace and Justice*.

In recent years a good number of Christians have become involved in the pro-life movement as a concrete expression of their commitment to justice. Surely the most vulnerable human being of all is the unborn infant; it needs protection from the violence of abortion. But thoughtful Christians come to the realization that they must extend this protection, as far as possible, to all of human life— including the handicapped, the chronically ill and the elderly. Moreover, following the lead of the U.S. bishops, they take a stand also against capital punishment and nuclear war. Cardinal Bernardin has called this consistent pro-life ethic "the seamless garment"—it is woven together in one piece.

I also think that pro-life activities must always be nonviolent. I do not see how pro-life people can justify physically harassing or verbally insulting women as they enter abortion clinics, much less bombing or torching the clinics themselves, as much as we might despise what goes on there. One of the most gospel-based approaches to abortion clinics that I have heard of is quietly going on in the Detroit area. A group of Christians goes out regularly in pairs (usually a man and a woman) to abortion clinics. They break no laws; they stand at the sidewalk as the woman approaches and say to her, "We'd like to ask you, for the love of God, to reconsider what you're going to do. Would you come and have coffee with us so we can talk?" If she accepts, they talk to her about alternatives to abortion and offer her medical and financial help if she needs it. I was struck by the courage and positiveness of this approach. The people told me they are surprised at how many girls and women really do not want the abortion and are grateful that someone can show them a realistic alternative.

Other Christians have become concerned about hunger, both in this country and in the world. They are not satisfied with working at soup kitchens or handing out food baskets, however necessary these may be. But they choose to look at the broader question of why people are hungry in the first place. Many of them join a national organization of Christians called "Bread for the World." They study the underlying causes of hunger and try to influence legislation and policies that will help reduce hunger by enabling people to feed themselves. As a matter of fact, Bread for the World has become a respected lobbying group on Capitol Hill. It's like the old saying, "Give a man a fish, and you'll keep him alive for a day. Teach him how to fish, and he'll keep himself alive."

Still other Christians are coming together around the issue of world peace. They have listened carefully to the prophetic call of Vatican II "to undertake a completely fresh reappraisal of war" (*The Church in the Modern World*, n. 80). They recall what Pope John XXIII said already in 1963 that "War is no longer an appropriate means of repairing injustice." They recall Vatican II's unequivocal condemnation of the arms race: "The arms race is one of the greatest curses on the human race, and the harm it inflicts on the poor is more than can be endured" (Ibid., n. 81). Some of them remember the powerful appearance of Pope Paul VI at the United Nations in 1965. On the feast of St. Francis of Assisi, the great peacemaker of medieval times, the pope stood up before the General Assembly and pleaded with all the representatives of the human family: "If you want to be brothers and sisters, let the weapons fall from your hands. You cannot love with weapons in your hands!" It was an electrifying moment.

In response to these urgent pleas, our American bishops have asked all Catholics to set aside every Friday, in memory of Jesus who gave his life in order to bring us together in peace, as a day of prayer, fasting and penance for peace. In addition, some Christians are making a private "Vow of Nonviolence" based on the Sermon on the Mount. (See complete text at the end of this chapter). Others have joined an international Catholic peace organization called Pax

Christi ("the Peace of Christ"), which works to educate people and to develop nonviolent strategies for peacemaking.

Finally, many Christians are working with church and civic groups to improve the quality of human life in whatever way they can: better schools, safer neighborhoods, cleaner air and water, the curbing of pornography. In doing so, they are convinced that they are doing God's work and are putting into practice the words of Jesus: "Amen, I say to you, whatever you did for one of these least brothers [and sisters] of mine, you did for me" (Mt 25:40).

I would like to conclude this chapter on responsibility by sharing an anecdote I heard about Mother Teresa of Calcutta. As you may know, she expects her sisters to spend their daytime hours going out and taking care of "the poorest of the poor." But in the evening they must spend at least an hour in prayer before the Blessed Sacrament. Once, when she was asked the reason for this, Mother Teresa answered, "Because you will never come to see Christ in the face of the poor if you do not spend time with him in adoration and prayer." That makes sense to me, and it is also my experience. So I want to say again: Our spirituality must always keep prayer and action together. If we do not spend time in regular prayer, we will not have the energy or creativity to meet our responsibilities without becoming tired or resentful. And, if our prayer does not lead us to take care of our loved ones and of our world, it will remain sterile. We cannot afford to separate what God has joined together.

VOW OF NONVIOLENCE

Recognizing the violence in my own heart, yet trusting in the goodness and mercy of God, I vow for one year to practice the nonviolence of Jesus who taught us in the Sermon on the Mount:

Blessed are the peacemakers, for they shall be called the sons and daughters of God. . . . You have learned how it was said, "You must love your neighbor and hate your enemy"; but I say to you, "Love your enemies, and pray for those who persecute you. In this way, you will be daughters and sons of your Creator in heaven."

Before God the Creator and the Sanctifying Spirit, I vow to carry out in my life the love and example of Jesus
- by striving for peace within myself and seeking to be a peacemaker in my daily life;

- by accepting suffering rather than inflicting it;
- by refusing to retaliate in the face of provocation and violence;
- by persevering in nonviolence of tongue and heart;
- by living conscientiously and simply so that I do not deprive others of the means to live;
- by actively resisting evil and working nonviolently to abolish war and the causes of war from my own heart and from the face of the earth.

God, I trust in your sustaining love and believe that just as you gave me the grace and desire to offer this, so you will also bestow abundant grace to fulfill it. (Copies of the Vow of Nonviolence may be obtained from Pax Christi USA, 348 E. 10th Street, Erie, PA 16503.)

7

Continuing Spiritual Growth

Throughout this book I have been making two basic assumptions. One is that, as I saw in that magazine article, "real men do have a spirituality." That is, there are a lot of males in our society who are not satisfied with pursuing The Great American Dream: wealth, status, success, power, or whatever. They either know intuitively or have learned by experience that the dream is more illusion than reality, at least in its capacity to provide genuine happiness and fulfillment. So these men are looking for something deeper, something they may not always name. But they know it has more to do with inner reality than with outward appearance, something more spiritual than material. We have named it "spirituality," and we defined it as "the ongoing endeavor to grow in our relationship with God." We saw that "spiritual growth" means forming a view of reality based on God's word in scripture and developing a lifestyle, making decisions, in light of that vision.

The second assumption is that spirituality is not just a head trip or a cozy feeling of being on good terms with God. It has to connect with and influence all the important aspects of a man's life. That's why we devoted whole chapters to the areas of work and leisure, friendship and marriage, and the exercise of responsibility. We tried to catch something of God's vision for these human realities and what kind of responses we may be called to make.

In this final chapter I will be making a third assumption: namely, that spirituality is never a once-and-for-all achievement. Rather, it is a process of ongoing growth, change and response to new challenges. It is dynamic rather than static. Just as nearly all workers today need continuing education in order to remain competent in their jobs, so every Christian needs continuing formation in order to grow toward spiritual maturity.

How does this happen? Classical Christian spirituality would answer: "through prayer and the sacraments." That is a good answer, and we have already considered these traditional means in earlier chapters. In Chapter 1 we saw that God takes the initiative in our spiritual life by offering us the gift of his friendship, and that our first response is to open our hearts to receive that gift. This includes a commitment on our part to bring all the parts of our life into harmony with God's way of seeing things and with his will for our lives. In Chapter 2 we saw that we cannot do this unless we regularly place ourselves in his presence through prayer, particularly by listening to his word in the scriptures. This is all the more important in our contemporary world because society is forever bombarding us with value messages that often contradict the spiritual vision God wants us to have. Then in Chapter 3, when we looked at our need for a good sense of self-worth, we considered the sacraments of reconciliation and the Eucharist as privileged ways of deepening our friendship with Jesus Christ and experiencing healing for our wounded self-image. I called these classical or traditional means of growing in the spiritual life. There are some others that I want to consider later.

Praying in Small Groups

Now, however, I would like to expand a bit on the practice of regular prayer. Ordinarily we think of prayer as a personal action, something we do in the silence and solitude of our own hearts. Indeed, this is the usual form our prayer will take. But some Christians today are finding a lot of help in prayer by occasionally joining with a small group for shared prayer. This is not a new practice, but one that goes back to the earliest days of Christianity. There is a strengthening effect when people give expression to their faith in the presence of others who support and affirm the same values.

For married Christians, one form this sometimes takes is what is called "couple prayer"—husband and wife praying together, not as individuals, but precisely as a couple. I came across a good description of this a few years ago in a magazine called *Praying*. It was an interview with a couple named Gene and Mary Lou Ott. They have been married for more than 20 years and have ten children, so you know they are not speaking out of an ivory tower! They began by saying that couple prayer has helped them realize something they didn't understand early in their marriage: namely, that when they began their marriage something new was created—their relationship. They described it as "almost like a third self" which not only nourishes them, but needs to be nourished by them.

When asked how they practice couple prayer, they said they've gone through a lot of trial and error and don't really have a clear five-step formula. But they emphasized that it's not that complicated: "Just begin, and develop your own style." What they do is simply invite the Lord into their relationship and then start talking. They begin by identifying what is going on within themselves: I'm happy about something that happened yesterday, or I'm sad or angry about something, or worried about something I have to face today or that I've noticed in one of the children. In other words, they begin with the "stuff" of daily life and of their relationship. They don't discuss it much or try to analyze it—they just name it and place it before the Lord and before each other. Then they read a passage of scripture, whatever part of the Bible they happen to be reading from at the time. After that they just sit in silence for awhile, letting that word of God touch their own lives. Then they share what has come to each of them while they were silent. They conclude with spontaneous prayers of thanksgiving and intercession.

"How often do you do this?" the interviewers asked. "We try to do it daily," Gene said, "between six and seven in the morning." Mary Lou must have seen a look of shock in the interviewers' faces, because she added, "We are parents of a big family. We don't have much time when we can go off by ourselves and not have the kids banging on the door. The children have always known that this is our time, that it's a sacred part of the day for us. . . . I feel like I am going to a well to get a drink of nourishment that gets me through the day." In other words, this couple puts a high priority on their prayer together.

When asked what would prevent other couples from trying this kind of thing, they replied that most couples have simply been unaware that it is possible and helpful; they've never been encouraged or "given permission" to try it. Mary Lou suggests they start with ten minutes a day; as it becomes more important to them, they will make more time for it. But they also realize that some people will be fearful of the honesty that this kind of prayer requires. As Gene said, "We may find we can't pray because we haven't talked out problems. We may have to say, 'Look, I can't pray because I'm upset with you. Can we talk?'" And Mary Lou added, "You can't fake prayer when you're sitting on a pile of garbage!" But they ended by saying that the intimacy they have found through prayer is more than worth any risks involved. Moreover, they have more peace about decisions they have to make because they always bring them before God and each other in prayer.

One of the values of couple prayer is that people experience a sense of support in their efforts to grow spiritually. But another way to find this is to become part of a group that gathers for prayer, scripture sharing, or dialogue together on Christian living. I think something like this is especially important for those who are single or who do not have the practice of praying as a couple. Again, this is something that is quite foreign to us Catholics. We have been brought up with the notion that our religion is a private matter, not something we talk about with others. In recent years, however, many Catholics have discovered the great value of sharing their faith in a small group setting. Some have done so through participation in diocesan-wide renewal programs such as Renew or Christ Renews His Parish. Others have simply been invited to join an informal group and found spiritual nourishment there. As you may recall from the Preface, this book grew out of my experiences of sharing with men who had made a retreat together on the stresses of midlife.

There are very few rules or guidelines for these groups. Most of them meet once a week or every two weeks. The ideal number is five to ten members. There doesn't have to be a leader, certainly not a priest. Practically any format can be followed, though generally there is some reading of scripture. The main idea is for people to talk about their own lives in the light of their faith. It is not a time for theological discussions or for griping about problems in the parish. It is a time for speaking, simply and honestly, about what this scripture passage says to me, about how I am finding the Lord (or not finding him) in my life, about how I responded well or poorly to the situations in which he placed me. If I have read or heard something that helped me or challenged me, I may want to share that with the group. People in the group learn to listen respectfully without judging, to encourage each other, sometimes to gently challenge each other to a deeper level of faith. And they learn to pray with and for each other and their loved ones. Many people have been helped through major crises in their lives by these kinds of groups, though they must not become a substitute for professional counseling when needed. The only times I have heard of people being hurt in these groups is when members become critical and judgmental of one another, or when one or two people dominate the group. Usually these things can be prevented if the group challenges them soon enough. My sense is that these faith-sharing groups are going to grow in importance as the society around us becomes more secularized and even hostile to spiritual values. We will need the face-to-face support of other believers if we are going to keep our spiritual vision clear.

Spiritual Growth

The question we have been considering in this chapter is: How do we continue to grow spiritually? I said that the classical, traditional answer to that question would be "through prayer and the sacraments." If the spiritual life is first and foremost a personal relationship with God in Jesus Christ, then we need to encounter him regularly in the ways he has provided for us. We also looked at two contemporary forms of prayer: praying as a couple and praying in small groups. At this point it would also be important to recall what we said at the end of the last chapter about working for peace and justice in the world. Our Catholic tradition has always held that Christian action, the practice of the Christian virtues, is another means of growing spiritually. Here is where some fundamentalist Christians will accuse us of believing that we are saved by our good works instead of by the grace of Christ. But that is a distortion of Catholic belief. We know very well that our own works are powerless to save us apart from what God has done for us in the death and resurrection of Jesus Christ. We believe what Paul stated so clearly, "For by grace you have been saved through faith, and this is not your own doing, it is the gift of God" (Eph 2:8). But we also believe what Paul said later in that same letter and in many other places: "Rather, living the truth in love, we should grow in every way into him who is the head, Christ" (Eph 4:15). "Live as children of the light, for light produces every kind of goodness and righteousness and truth. Try to learn what is pleasing to the Lord" (Eph 5:8-10).

All the New Testament writers are clear that the Christian life is not merely a matter of rejoicing that we are saved in Christ. It is also an ongoing struggle to bring all of our personal life and our relationships under the direction of the Holy Spirit, the Spirit of Jesus. That means constant conversion, saying no to our self-centered desires and yes to the requirements of the gospel and the needs of our brothers and sisters. Each time we do that, we are growing in our relationship with the Lord. We are saying, in a concrete way, that his will and his king-dom mean more to us than anything else in life. "Continue," Paul says, "to live in Christ Jesus the Lord, in the spirit in which you received him [that is, when you first accepted him and committed yourself to him]. Be rooted in him and built up in him, growing ever stronger in the faith" (Col 2:6-7). That sounds a lot like "spiritual growth."

Spiritual Growth Through Ministry

As we saw in the last chapter, the documents of the church, es-pecially in Vatican II, envision the vocation of the laity as being acted out primarily in the arena of the secular world.

> By the daily example of their Christian lives and by whatever influence they are able to have, the laity work to transform the secular world in accord with God's plan for human betterment: By their competence in secular disciplines and by their activity, let the laity work earnestly in order that created goods through human labor, technical skill and civil culture may serve to bene-fit all people according to the plan of the creator and the light of his word. . . . Thus . . . will Christ increasingly illuminate the whole of human society with his saving light (*Dogmatic Consti-tution on the Church*, n. 36).

However, since the council another dimension of the lay voca-tion has become more and more apparent—what is often called Christian service or "ministry." Lay people are becoming more aware that the church itself needs their gifts and their services. Cer-tainly one impetus for this has been the dramatic decrease in the number of priests and religious, which is leaving large gaps in the church's ministry and outreach. But necessity sometimes also leads us to the rediscovery of some forgotten or neglected truth. In this case, it has served to remind us that ministry and service are the vocation of the entire church, not just the bishops, priests and religious.

The early church simply took this for granted. Peter wrote to the Christians of his time, "As each one has received a gift, use it to serve one another as good stewards of God's varied grace" (1 Pt 4:10). Paul reminded the Roman and Corinthian believers that each of them had some gift or talent that could help build up the entire community in

Christ (Rom 12:4-8; 1 Cor 12:4-11). His letter to the Romans ends with special greetings to lay Christians, women as well as men, who were ministering in the church there: the married couple Prisca and Aquila, "my co-workers in Christ Jesus" (Rom 16:3); Andronicus and Junias, who were imprisoned with Paul and are now "prominent among the apostles" (16:7); Tryphaena and Tryphosa, "those workers in the Lord: and also to dear Persis, who worked hard for the Lord" (16:12). Throughout Paul's other letters there are references to individual Christians who were exercising some sort of ministry in the local church communities.

As a matter of fact, the Second Vatican Council sees participation in the church's ministry not as something extraordinary for the laity but as something that flows directly from their baptism and confirmation. Through these sacraments, the council says, "all are appointed to this apostolate by the Lord himself" (*Dogmatic Constitution on the Church*, n. 33). Which means that bishops and priests have no right to "keep the laity in their place"—that is, quiet, passive and uninvolved. If "all are appointed by the Lord himself" to share in the church's ministry, then the pastor's task is to call forth the gifts of the laity and to empower them to work together for the good of the entire community. Which is why the council asks that "the way be clear for the laity to share diligently in the saving work of the Church according to their ability and the needs of the times" (n. 33).

This is the biblical and theological background for what we see happening in the church today: men being ordained as permanent deacons, men and women being trained in other ministries such as lector, eucharistic minister, and catechist. Some of the men I have met are finding a great deal of fulfillment in the exercise of these ministries. They don't just get up and read the scriptures at Mass haphazardly; they pray over the word of God ahead of time, they digest it personally and then they proclaim it with power and conviction. When they minister the consecrated bread and wine, it is evident that they really believe they are inviting you to share in the body and blood of Jesus Christ. When they bring the Eucharist to the sick or shut-ins, they make it a point to listen to the person, to pray with him or her and to bring something of the parish's care and concern into that person's life. I marvel at how some catechists keep giving their best week after week, sometimes to a group of unresponsive kids, because the catechist is so convinced of the truths of our faith.

But these are not the only forms of ministry. I have dealt with a lot of men who are involved in their parish councils or commissions. They know they have something positive to contribute, even when it is not always appreciated. Some men and their wives assist the pastor in preparing engaged couples for the sacrament of matrimony. Today no pastor or pastoral team can expect to have expertise in every area that affects parish life; and they certainly can't expect to do everything themselves. The help of the laity is absolutely indispensable.

But a word of caution here. I have seen some people get carried away by trying to serve within the church. They invest so much of their time and energy that they have almost nothing to give to their spouse and children. That is unbalanced. It is certainly not a sign of healthy spirituality. Our primary commitments have to remain primary. It is just as wrong for a man to get overinvolved in church work as in any other kind of work. A couple of years ago Dolores Curran wrote an article for *U.S. Catholic* entitled "Religion Is Ruining Our Marriage." She showed how religion, which ought to be a bonding force between couples, can sometimes become divisive instead. She told about one wife who thinks her husband should have been a priest. "He is constantly off making and giving retreats," she complained, "spending more time with clergy than with family." She went on to describe the great strain this has placed on family relationships. Sometimes this kind of "gung-ho" commitment to church work can be a way of avoiding problems in marital or family relationships, and either spouse (or both) may resort to it. But it is a distortion. Our spirituality must always be balanced and integrated with the rest of our lives.

Apart from these more visible ministries, there are a great number of men whose service is more hidden and behind the scenes. I'm thinking of people like ushers, or the fellows who set up tables and chairs for parish functions, or work at the fish fries. I'm thinking of the men who get involved with the youth of the parish—helping on retreats, camping trips and athletic events. I'm thinking of a couple of fellows I know who have a gift of music; they not only help at the Sunday liturgies, but they go around playing and singing at nursing homes and for gatherings of youth. I'm thinking of several retired and semi-retired men at a retreat center who save the place thousands of dollars a year by helping with the maintenance of the building and grounds. Moreover, I believe there are gifts and ministries around that we haven't even begun to tap. For example, we often hear that bartenders listen to more confessions and problems than most priests and psychiatrists. Why couldn't we give some training in "the art of Christian listening" to lay people who seem to have the natural gift, and let them be available for people who need someone to talk to in a perspective of faith?

Call to Evangelization

Which brings me to my next point. It seems to me that we Catholic Christians have not been all that good at using either our ears or our mouths. I have always thought that one of the most instructive gestures in the rite of baptism is when the priest touches the ears and mouth of the person and says, "The Lord Jesus made the deaf hear and the mute speak. May he soon touch your ears to receive his word, and your mouth to proclaim his faith." But for a long time we Catholics were reluctant to listen to the people of other faiths because we thought we had all the answers. We are getting better at that now, thanks to the spirit of ecumenism. But we are still reluctant to speak to others about what we believe.

Lately I have been paying a lot of attention to the last words of Jesus recorded in the gospels. According to Matthew, Jesus gathers the apostles together and addresses them in solemn words:

> "All power in heaven and earth has been given to me. Go, therefore, and make disciples of all nations, baptizing them in the name of the Father, and of the Son, and of the holy Spirit, teaching them to observe all that I have commanded you. And behold, I am with you always, until the end of the age" (Mt 28:18-20).

The words are similar in the gospel of Mark (16:15-16), and of Luke (24:46-49). This scene is often called "the great commissioning." Jesus makes it clear that the church does not exist for its own sake. It has a mission, a purpose. It must not let the world forget Jesus Christ. It must continue to make him known and to proclaim his teachings everywhere in the world until time is no more.

That's what Peter, Paul and the other apostles tried to do with tireless energy. That's why the church continues to send out missionaries in every age. That's why our ancestors, when they settled in this country, made great sacrifices to build churches and schools: They wanted to preserve their faith and to hand it on to the next generations. Their families and friends in Europe were convinced that the new settlers would lose their faith in this wild and pagan land. But what happened? They not only preserved the faith, but they built a strong and vibrant American church.

That much is history. Today, however, the Catholic church appears to be losing some of its vitality. Numerically there are more Catholics than ever, but the level of participation and involvement is slipping. Polls show that weekly Mass attendance among Catholics has fallen—from over 70 percent in 1963 to less than 50 percent in 1985. Moreover, many pastors report that only a small percentage of their parishioners are involved in parish life outside of Sunday Mass. Another symptom: In the last two years the number of adult converts to the faith has declined by 7.7 percent; we are now at the lowest ratio of converts to active Catholics in the history of the church in this country. An even more serious symptom: Large numbers of Catholics are either leaving the church or becoming inactive. Research now indicates that there are about 15 million non-practicing Catholics in the United States today—some 26 percent of all baptized Catholics. The problem is especially acute among young adults, age 18-30; nearly 50 percent of them leave the church. Any organization with that kind of dropout rate cannot afford to be complacent. To round out the picture, we are told that there are at least 80 million people in this country who have no church connection whatever. This would mean that about one of every three Americans is unchurched.

The point is, there are vast numbers of people in this country who are not being touched by the gospel of Christ. "A sleeping giant" is the image that some people are using to describe the modern Catholic church. That is, it has enormous strength and potential, but it seems dormant or paralyzed right now.

As a matter of fact, this has been a matter of serious concern for some years, not only in this country but worldwide. That's why, in 1974, Pope Paul VI convened the Third Synod of Bishops in Rome on the theme of "evangelization." He challenged the bishops from around the world to deal with what he called three "burning questions":

—In our day, what has happened to that hidden energy of the gospel, which is able to have a powerful effect on people's minds?

—To what extent and in what way is that evangelical force capable of really transforming the people of this century?

—What methods should be followed in order that the power of the gospel may have its effect?

The pope was clearly concerned. He knew that there is great power in the gospel of Christ to answer the needs and longings of the people of the present age; but somehow the message wasn't getting through. When the bishops got through with their discussions, they asked the pope himself to write a document that would not only summarize their deliberations but would be a fresh appeal to the church everywhere to take up the task of proclaiming the gospel with renewed vigor.

Encyclical on Evangelization

Paul VI responded with his Apostolic Exhortation entitled *Evangelization in the Modern World*, dated December 8, 1975, exactly ten years after the close of Vatican II. I want to say that no other papal document has moved me as much as this one. Most of them are lofty and beautiful, but they're pretty dry. This one is on fire with passion and enthusiasm. It is practical, hard-hitting, challenging. It appeals to our hearts as well as our minds, and it makes us want to do everything we can to bring the gospel of Christ to the people of our time. Unfortunately, I'm afraid the document has been largely ignored. Maybe one reason is that we Catholics are not comfortable with the word "evangelization." It sounds vaguely "Protestant," or it evokes negative images of television evangelists. In reality, evangelization is steeped in our Catholic tradition. It simply means bringing the good news of the gospel to people so that they will come to know Jesus Christ and try to live his teachings. Paul VI says that is what constitutes the very mission and purpose of the church, its deepest identity. The church "exists in order to evangelize," he says, "in order to preach and teach, to be the channel of the gift of grace, to reconcile sinners with God . . ." (n. 14).

One of the major points the pope makes in his letter is that *every person in the world has a right to hear the gospel*. This flows from the command of Jesus to "Go, therefore, and make disciples of all the nations" (Mt. 28:18). For the church, then, the presentation of the gospel message is not an option. "This message is indeed necessary," the pope says. "It is unique. It cannot be replaced. . . . It is a question of people's salvation. . . . It brings with it a wisdom that is not of this world. It is able by itself to stir up faith—faith that rests on the power of God" (n. 5). Now if it is true that all people have a basic right to hear the good news about Jesus Christ, then the church must make it known to them, even if they do not ask for it. That's why the church sends out missionaries to every land. We surely have no right to impose the gospel on anyone, but at least we must expose them to it so that they are able to make a choice. Just how this is to be done, of course, remains a matter of good judgment and of sensitivity to other beliefs and cultures. It was interesting to see how Pope John Paul II did this during his recent visit to Japan. At one point he addressed a group of Buddhists, Shintoists and other non-Christian religious leaders. I don't remember his exact words, but he said something like this: "I have studied your religions and have been moved by the truth and beauty I find in them. But now—I must also tell you about Jesus Christ." And he went on to give them a summary of the gospel, without any criticism or put-down of their own religions.

Pope Paul VI makes another strong point in his letter on evangelization: *Every baptized Christian is called to spread the gospel.* "The whole church is called upon to evangelize," he says, not just the bishops and priests (n. 66). Here is where some Catholics may balk. They are not used to thinking of themselves as evangelizers; that's something for those "offbeat" groups like the Mormons and Jehovah's Witnesses. But we Catholics have been taught for years that our religion is pretty much a private matter—something between ourselves and God, and you don't "wear it on your sleeve" except maybe in church. Yet Paul VI says: "The person who has been evangelized goes on to evangelize others. Here lies the test of truth . . . ; it is unthinkable that a person would accept the Word (of God) and give himself to the Kingdom (of God) without becoming a person who bears witness to it and proclaims it in turn" (n. 24).

Think of the early Christians: They simply took it for granted that the good news had to be shared. I imagine things happening something like this: People heard the first apostles preach about Jesus and they witnessed the "signs and wonders" (healings and expulsion of demons) that accompanied their preaching. They asked for baptism and became Christians. Then they would go out and meet their family and friends, who would say to them, "What's happened to you? You've changed." And the new Christian would say, "You're right—I've come to know Jesus Christ!" And the friend or family member would say, "Tell me about him." That's how the Christian faith spread. There weren't a lot of mass conversions; there were many more of these one-to-one connections between people. That's why in his letters St. Paul so often praises the Christians for the fact that "the word of the Lord has echoed forth from you resoundingly" (1 Thes 1:8) and that their faith is being talked about everywhere. Clearly these Christians were not just keeping the faith, they were spreading it; and Paul was proud of them. I like to paraphrase one of his statements to the effect that "we are the good fragrance of Christ in a stinky world" (see 2 Cor 2:14-15).

But now, a problem: How can we be effective evangelizers without turning people off? (One tape I listened to has the intriguing title: "How to evangelize without becoming obnoxious"!) I'm sure many of us have had the experience of people trying to "convert us to the Lord" at the most inappropriate times and with ungraceful manners. We surely don't want to swell the ranks of those folks.

I think the first thing we need to do is to develop the outlook and attitude of Jesus. Matthew's gospel has a scene which I find very instructive. He says:

> Jesus went around to the towns and villages, teaching in their synagogues, proclaiming the gospel of the kingdom, and curing every disease and illness. At the sight of the crowds, his heart was moved with pity for them because they were troubled and abandoned, like sheep without a shepherd (Mt 9:35-36).

The Old Testament prophets, particularly Jeremiah and Ezekiel, had also pictured God's people as sheep who were "scattered" or "wandering aimlessly." The image is that of people who are spiritually hungry and desolate. What did Jesus do? He asked the disciples to pray that God may send "laborers" (evangelists) to help them. Then he empowered the disciples themselves to bring the good news of the gospel to those who are spiritually exhausted (Mt 9:37-10:7).

Now, can we let our mind turn to those 15 million inactive Catholics, and those 80 million unchurched people, and try to see them as Jesus does? Can we let our hearts be moved with compassion? Indeed, can we take them into our heart and try to love them as he does? Only if we do that will we be able to avoid the pitfalls of obnoxious evangelism. Otherwise, we will be tempted to view them as potential "conquests," or as numbers to fill up our churches, or as poor sinners whom we need to "save" in order to make ourselves feel good. That is why there can be no true evangelization apart from prayer. We need to pray to have the vision of Jesus, to be purified of our needs for power or dominance, and to remember that it is not we ourselves but the Holy Spirit who is the true agent of evangelization. As Pope Paul VI said, "We exhort all evangelizers, whoever they may be, to pray without ceasing to the Holy Spirit with faith and fervor, and to let themselves prudently be guided by him as the decisive inspirer of their plans, their initiatives and their evangelizing activity" (n. 75).

Ways of Evangelizing

Well, granted that we are praying for the proper attitude and spirit of evangelization, how do we actually do it? First let's be clear about something: We're not talking about trying to make Catholic converts out of people who are already committed to another Christian faith. We are concerned about those people who are "wandering aimlessly," who are disconnected from any church community. How can we evangelize them?

Pope Paul VI suggests two approaches. Above all, he says, the gospel must be proclaimed by the "wordless witness" of our lives—that is, by our example of Christian living. The very quality of our lives—our generosity and willingness to share, our thoughtfulness of others, our cheerfulness, our striving for excellence in our work, our devotion to family, our rejection of violence, racism and sexism—all this will be noticed by people and will stir up deeper questions within them: What is their secret? What is the source of their energy, their serenity? "Such a witness," the pope says, "is already a silent proclamation of the Good News, and a very powerful and effective one . . . an initial act of evangelization" (n. 21).

Some examples immediately come to my mind. Bob Greene, a columnist in *The Chicago Tribune*, once printed a story about a doctor who sent a printed card along with the bill that came to his patients. He always stated the full fee for his services, but the card said that if anyone had a serious hardship in paying the bill, the doctor would accept a reduced fee: "I suggest a 25 percent reduction, but more or less may be appropriate to your situation. No discussion is necessary . . . simply write the amount of fee reduction you choose on the statement with your remittance."

Bob Greene called him for an interview, but the doctor made it clear that he did not want his name published. Greene was surprised, considering how most people today would give anything for media attention. He suggested maybe the doctor feared he would be swamped by too many patients. But the doctor laughed at his cynicism. "No," he said, "I can pretty well control the size of my own practice. But you see, if I started getting publicity about it, I would have to question my own motives. I would always wonder if I was really doing it for my patients after all." Greene asked him if he didn't consider his attitude unusual. "I don't know," the doctor replied. "Frankly, I'm in pretty good financial shape. I know some of my patients aren't. So this just seems like the right thing to do."

I was touched. So was Bob Greene. At the end he wrote, "Here's to you, doctor; here's to you. And may your specialness reward you in ways that matter to you. In the end, that's all that counts anyway."

I have no way of knowing whether the doctor was a Christian or not. But to me he is a symbol of all the men I have met whose lives bear witness to their belief in the values of Jesus Christ. I think of the recovering alcoholics who will go out at any hour of the day or night to talk with a fellow alcoholic who is struggling with his addiction. I think of the men who have turned down great job promotions, because they knew it would interfere with family life. I think of the men who give up some of their favorite recreations in order to help kids who wouldn't otherwise have a chance for any wholesome activity. Like the doctor in Bob Greene's column, they don't want any publicity or recognition; it "just seems like the right thing to do."

However, Paul VI goes on to say, this "silent witness" is not sufficient for evangelization: "The Good News proclaimed by the *witness* of life must sooner or later be proclaimed by the *word* of life" (n. 22). At some point we are called upon to speak of what we believe, to make Jesus Christ known explicitly. How do we know when to do this? There are no rules for it, as far as I know. I like evangelist John Wimber's notion of "divine appointments." That is, at times it will be obvious that God has set you up in a situation where you just know it's the right thing to speak about your faith in Christ. I heard about a Catholic man who works in the credit department of a bank. He says he often talks to people in financial crisis, which leads them to open up a great deal of their personal lives to him. He is a prayerful man, and he says there are times when he just knows he should say something like, "Well, friend, I can certainly arrange a loan for you. But from what you've told me, there are areas of your life that are in disarray. May I ask if you are a Christian?" If the person says yes, he goes on, "Have you ever brought any of this to prayer? Have you ever put it before the Lord and asked him to help you see and deal with it in a better way?" Then he goes on to share with the person how he himself has experienced God's help in his own life problems.

I'm really convinced that anyone can be an evangelizer. You don't need a soapbox; you don't need to go around ringing doorbells; you don't have to be an eloquent speaker. There are really only three "techniques" we need for good evangelization: listening, sharing our story and inviting. Let's look a little closer at each one.

Tools for Evangelizing

First, listening. The great Lutheran pastor and theologian Dietrich Bonhoeffer once wrote that since the love of God begins with listening to his word, so the beginning of love of neighbor is learning to listen to them: "Christians too often are busy talking when they should be listening. They have forgotten that the ministry of listening is committed to them by the One who is himself the greatest listener. We should listen with the ears of God, so that we may speak the word of God."

I like that. I especially like the notion of listening as a "ministry." It's a sad commentary on our times that people often can't find anyone who will listen to them—with sincere interest, without making quick judgments and without giving flippant advice or easy solutions to complex problems. In the context of evangelization, listening means that we take time to hear people out before we start talking to them about God. It means drawing them out, inviting them to tell their story—of hurt, of pain, of broken dreams, of disappointed hopes.

For instance, a fellow tells you that he "got rid of religion" when he went to college because he finally realized that his rigid religious upbringing had messed him up psychologically. Yet, as you listen, you detect an ambivalence about this: He is glad that the God of his childhood is dead, but there is now a vacuum in his life that wants to be filled. So you gently suggest that maybe he is still searching for some religious connection with his life. He agrees, and before long you are talking with him about the God you have come to believe in. All because you took the time to listen. Or a former Catholic tells you that she became fed up with the church when the pastor refused to marry her daughter in church because the daughter had no intention of practicing her faith. Instead of rushing to the defense of the pastor, your listening enables you to hear a deeper theme: the woman's own feeling of guilt and self-blame for her daughter's loss of faith. Her tone of anger and bitterness turns to a request for help to find some kind of reconciliation with her wounded self and with the church. I know full well that listening alone does not always work such marvels; but I also know that very little that is constructive will happen without good listening.

After we have taken the time to listen, the next step in evangelizing is to give our own testimony—that is, to share with the person something of our own experience of searching for God and finding him in the concrete realities of our life. To the fellow who thought that his childhood religion had messed him up, for instance, we might share the fact that we had gone through a period of doubt or denial ourselves, that our childish faith had to die in order for us to come to an adult understanding of God. We may go on to share how this new level of faith has enabled us to find peace and strength in dealing with our problems. To alienated Catholics we might say, "Yes, I have my own anger and disappointment with the church. But I came to realize that I was only hurting myself by dropping out. I still don't like some things, but I'm finding more positive than negative. And I'm seeing that the church needs my input if it's going to continue growing." The details have to be filled in, and the exact words aren't important. What's important is that we speak from our own experience, not from theology books, and that we somehow connect with the other person's experience.

Above all, we avoid argumentation. We don't need to defend God or the church. They can take care of themselves. If the other person becomes defensive or wants to argue, it is usually a sign that they are not yet ready to hear another viewpoint. So we simply back off, and entrust them to the Lord. Chances are, they will think about what we said, especially if they are really searching. So the seed of the good news we have planted will grow in its own good time (see Mk 4:26-27).

This leads to our third "technique" for evangelization: inviting. If the person has shown some interest in what we have to say, or if they keep asking questions, we may share as much of the gospel message as they seem ready for. But then we extend an invitation:

"I have a good booklet that you might find helpful; would you like to borrow it?"

"Would you like to come with us to Mass next Sunday?"

"We have a Bible Study group that meets every week—would you like to join us next time?"

"Our parish has a great adult education program going right now—how about going with us?"

"I know a good priest you could talk to about some of the questions you're bringing up."

Above all, don't leave people hanging, even if they turn down invitations. At least ask if you can contact them again in a week or so to see how they're doing. If they refuse, of course, you will certainly want to respect that. The beauty of the invitational approach is that it is non-coercive and non-threatening.

What I have just presented here is a highly condensed summary of a whole training program in the theory and practice of evangelization that I will be developing over the next few years. I have included it here under the topic of spiritual growth for this reason: Evangelization and spiritual growth interact to form a positive upward spiral. That is, when I open up to the Lord and begin to catch his vision of life, I become energized and want to share it with others. When I do that, and find that they become energized, I am moved to open up even more and to grow deeper in my relationship with him. I have found this to be consistently true in my own life, and I have heard it expressed by so many Christians whom I have come to know.

Retreat for Spiritual Growth

There is one last means of spiritual growth that I would like to single out—what is generally called a "retreat." It is based on the need that Christians have often felt to get away from the ordinary preoccupations of their lives and to spend some time reflecting on the quality of their spiritual life, their relationship with God. For centuries, priests and religious have been obliged to do this by law, because it was assumed to be necessary in order not to burn out or dry up spiritually. But lay Christians have often felt the same need. In fact, the first retreat centers in this country were begun at the request of Catholic laymen who approached their bishops and asked for help in getting a place started.

A typical retreat takes place on a weekend, starting Friday night and closing Sunday afternoon. It consists mainly of listening to spiritual conferences and reflecting on them in the light of one's own life. Sometimes the topic is discussed in small groups, but often there is silence during the entire retreat. Each retreatant usually has a private room. The retreat directors are available for private consultation if desired. And the retreatants participate in the liturgies and other prayer services.

It doesn't sound like much, but the impact can be powerful. I had never worked out of a retreat center until three years ago. Before that I had been a teacher and a counselor for about 20 years. I had the idea that people who make retreats are kind of an elite group, people who pretty well have their lives together and are coming to have the wrinkles in their souls ironed out. But my eyes were opened. I discovered that retreatants cover the whole range of the Catholic population, and I learned that some Protestant Christians also come for retreats.

Retreatants include men and women of all age groups and economic groups. They are single, married, widowed and divorced. Some have reached a depth of spirituality that inspires and humbles me. Some have made a good beginning, but are struggling to keep their balance in a world that makes heavy demands on them. Some have recently been touched by the Lord and are coming for the first time because they want to know him more deeply. Some have been wounded by the shocks and hurts of life and are in need of healing. Some have lost the faith of their childhood but are searching for something to believe in.

Week after week, as I listen to our retreatants' stories, I am in awe at the mystery of divine grace at work in the depths of their souls. Suddenly the great themes of the Bible come alive before my eyes: God in search of his human creatures; our resistance and our guilt; our fear of rejection and failure; our need to forgive ourselves and each other for our mistakes; the peace and quiet joy that can be ours if we surrender ourselves to God's transforming love. And I have become aware that the distance between myself and the retreatants is paper-thin. I am their priest; but even more, I am their fellow Christian trying to walk the way of discipleship in the company of Jesus.

Something else happens on a retreat that is beautiful to watch: It is not our words that touch the retreatants, but the word of God. As we invite them to reflect on the scriptures in silence and in prayer, they find nourishment for their own spirit, for their particular circumstances. They find a new way to view their problems and new strength to deal with them. They find confirmation and encouragement for the directions they have taken. They see how their faith can touch their work, their relationships, their role as parents. They find healing for their wounds and release from their anxieties. And sometimes they find challenge to reverse the direction their life is taking, because it does not measure up to the gospel. As one man told me, "The retreat helped me to come home to myself. Now I feel free to open that home to others"— whereas before he had been drowning himself in work and shutting people out because he was afraid to look honestly at himself.

I'm not saying that retreats are absolutely essential for spiritual growth. But I know that for many Christians today, an annual retreat is becoming as normal for their spiritual growth as an annual vacation is for their mental health. I also know that I would never have had the motivation to write this book if I had not met so many men on retreats who are hungry for a deeper spirituality and looking for some guidance on their spiritual journey.

So there we have it. Spiritual growth is the process of bringing more and more of our daily life into harmony with the gospel vision of Jesus Christ and the plan of God for our true fulfillment. We grow by "paying attention to the presence of God" (our definition of prayer) in the scriptures and in daily events. That's why we pray and participate in the church's sacraments—to keep our vision clear and to stay in touch with our source of energy. We also grow by extending ourselves in action. We saw that our occupations themselves can be ways of contributing to the fulfillment of God's plan for a more just and human world. Some of us may be called to work directly in some form of ministry within the church, in various ways of serving the needs of our brothers and sisters. Finally, we reflected on Christ's call to evangelization, to share the good news we have come to treasure with the people in our environment.

Final Reflections

As I told people about this manuscript, one of the questions they sometimes asked was, "Why are you writing a book like that just for men? Don't women need to develop a spirituality too?" My answer is that they certainly do. But my experience is that there is quite an abundance of good spiritual literature for women nowadays, but very little for men. I believe this is a serious gap which needs to be filled. There are too many men sensing a need for spiritual nourishment and do not know where to look for it. At the same time, I am aware that many of the reflections in this book will apply to women as well, as my two women typists have assured me.

In Chapter 1, I described three types of Christians: "cradle-to-adult" Christians, "lost-and-found" Christians and "up-from-crisis" Christians. Now I would like to add a fourth category: "seekers." I believe that many of you readers will fit more comfortably in this last category. You may be right in the middle of the first three, or not quite in any of them. But in any case, you are vaguely dissatisfied with the quality of your life. You sense that something is missing, and you feel at least some desire for spiritual growth and for a better relationship with God.

What I have tried to show in this book is that your seeking is neither foolish nor doomed to failure. As I have said, God takes the initiative in searching for us; our job is to open ourselves to his presence and activity in our lives. The careful research of the great psychologist Abraham Maslow led him to the conclusion that religious beliefs and values have great potential for promoting psychic health and personal maturity. In his famous study of "self-actualizing" people (who showed an extraordinary degree of wholeness and creativity), he found that every one of them had a belief in a meaningful universe and a life which could be called spiritual, even though many were not "religious" in the orthodox sense of the word. This is another testimony that nature and grace, holiness and wholeness, belong together.

As we have seen, spirituality is not just for the elite but for anyone who wants to live more deeply and fully. It is not dull, because it is centered in our relationship with God, who is always surprising us by showing us something new. It is not for wimps, because it calls for discipline and generosity. Spirituality has the potential to release the most creative energies within human nature and to bring us to the deepest satisfactions of which we are capable. Indeed, real men (and women) do have a spirituality.

As you, my readers, continue on your own spiritual journey, may you find many good companions on the way.

Suggested Resources

Barbeau, Clayton. *Delivering the Male* (San Francisco, CA: Harper & Row, 1982)

Conway, Jim. *Men in Midlife Crisis* (Elgin, IL: David C. Cook, 1978)

Curran, Dolores. *Traits of a Healthy Family* (San Francisco, CA: Harper & Row, 1983)

Dobson, James. *Dare to Discipline* (Wheaton, IL: Tyndale House, 1970)

   Straight Talk to Men and Their Wives (Waco, TX: Word Books, 1980)

McGinnis, James and Kathleen. *Parenting for Peace and Justice* (Maryknoll, NY: Orbis Books, 1981)

Powell, John. *The Secret of Staying in Love* (Allen, TX: Tabor Publishing, 1984)

   A Christian Vision (Allen, TX: Tabor Publishing, 1984)

Peck, M. Scott. *The Road Less Traveled* (New York, NY: Simon & Schuster, 1978)

Rohr, O.F.M., Richard. "A Man's Approach to God" tape series (Cincinnati, OH: St. Anthony Messenger Press, 1978)

CRITZ
CONT
ALB
sueen
deliverd

22 MEN ON 6/12
10 MEN ON 6/19

12 MEN ON 7/1

15 MEN ON 7/10